D0214219

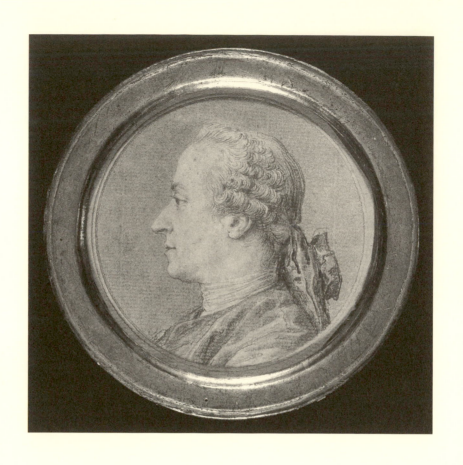

Essay on Gardens

A Chapter in the French Picturesque

TRANSLATED INTO ENGLISH FOR THE FIRST TIME

CLAUDE-HENRI WATELET

Edited and Translated by Samuel Danon

Introduction by Joseph Disponzio

PENN

University of Pennsylvania Press

Philadelphia

PENN STUDIES IN LANDSCAPE ARCHITECTURE
John Dixon Hunt, Series Editor
This series is dedicated to the study and promotion of a wide variety of approaches to landscape architecture, with special emphasis on connections between theory and practice. It includes monographs on key topics in history and theory, descriptions of projects by both established and rising designers, translations of major foreign-language texts, anthologies of theoretical and historical writings on classic issues, and critical writing by members of the profession of landscape architecture.

Copyright © 2003 University of Pennsylvania Press
All rights reserved
Printed in the United States of America on acid-free paper

10 9 8 7 6 5 4 3 2 1

Published by
University of Pennsylvania Press
Philadelphia, Pennsylvania 19104-4011

Library of Congress Cataloging-in-Publication Data

Watelet, Claude-Henri, 1718–1786.
    [Essai sur les jardins. English]
    Essay on gardens : a chapter in the French picturesque translated into English for the first time / Claude-Henri Watelet ; edited and translated by Samuel Danon ; introduction by Joseph Disponzio.
        p.   cm. — (Penn studies in landscape architecture)
    Includes bibliographical references (p.).
    ISBN 0-8122-3722-6 (cloth : alk. paper)
    1. Gardens—France—History—18th century. 2. Gardens, French—History—18th century. 3. Picturesque, The. I. Danon, Samuel, 1937–. II. Title. III. Series.
SB466.F8 W3813   2003
712'.6'094409033—dc21   2002040932

Frontispiece: Claude-Henri Watelet. Pencil drawing by Charles-Nicolas Cochin. Private collection.

Contents

Introduction

JOSEPH DISPONZIO

Claude-Henri Watelet's *Essai sur les jardins* (*Essay on Gardens*) has long been a staple in the study of the picturesque garden in France. Its brevity belies its impact on the aesthetics of sensibility of the eighteenth century, especially as they directed the conception and development of picturesque gardening in pre-Revolutionary France. Yet, outside the small circle of scholars, it is a work little appreciated and seldom considered.[1] Its obscurity has less to do with its artistic merit than with those who have written the history of the French picturesque, as well as the ambivalence the French have had for an art form tainted by a foreign import—the English garden. Fortunately, the history of the French contribution to the development of the *jardin anglais* (English garden) is in the process of being rewritten, and Watelet's *Essay* occupies a central place within it.[2]

Watelet himself is somewhat better known than his garden essay. Born in Paris on August 28, 1718, he became a fixture in academic, artistic, and *philosophes* circles. He died in his native city some sixty-eight years later on January 12, 1786, having lived a charmed life of privilege, which if not standard for a man of his station, was enhanced by his innate gifts for aesthetic pleasures. He was born rich, considerably so. His father was a *receveur général des finances*—somewhat like a regional tax collector—a royal sinecure Watelet inherited, along with his father's fortune, at age twenty-two. With his livelihood secure, but with no particular penchant or aptitude for finance, Watelet embarked on a life of refined leisure devoted to the beaux arts. As was appropriate for someone of his avocation and wealth, he took young artists under his wing, frequented and supported the intellectual and artistic *salon* culture of the day, and was a host of considerable charm and generosity. His friends and acquaintances, drawn from the upper levels of pre-Revolutionary Parisian society, included both artists and arbiters of taste, among them François Boucher, Jean-Baptiste Greuze, Abel-François Poisson, marquis de Marigny, and Anne-Claude-Philippe, comte de Caylus.

Although a bachelor, he lived intimately with his mistress, Marguerite Le Comte, a woman of considerable artistic accomplishment in her own right. Having a mistress during the Old Regime was common practice, but Watelet's ménage was, if not singular, at least special. For the forty or so years that they were together, most of which was lived under the same roof, they shared company with Mme Le Comte's husband, Jacques-Roger Le Comte. Presumably, Watelet was devoted to his mistress and treated her husband impeccably, for by all contemporary accounts, they lived in respectful, if not peaceful, conjugality, one degree—or bed—removed. All three profited from the situation: the lovers with each other, the husband enjoying companionship without connubial responsibility. They even traveled together, most notably on a celebrated trip to Italy in 1763–1764, culminating in a lavish party given in their honor by the French Academy in Rome. The visit was immortalized in an elegant suite of engravings produced by students of the Academy, set to a poem by Louis Subleyras and drawings by, among others, Hubert Robert.[3] In illustration and verse, the visit is recounted through allegory and classical imagery, including a flattering apotheosis of Mme Le Comte being crowned by Apollo, Watelet at her side. The entire work is as much a commemoration of a Grand Tour as a sumptuous album of an enduring and highly compatible love affair.

In addition to his mastery of the etiquette of the day, Watelet distinguished himself in the beaux arts, something for which he had affinity. On his first trip to Rome at eighteen, his talents as a draftsman were recognized by the French Academy, which invited him to participate in drawing classes. In 1747 he became an associate member of the Royal Academy of Painting and Sculpture, the first of numerous artistic and learned societies to which he was elected, including—in addition to the most important French academies—those of Berlin, Cordoba, Florence, Madrid, Parma, Rome, and Vienna. Watelet was an accomplished poet, playwright, painter, sculptor, engraver, and musician as well as an art connoisseur. His private collection was considerable and included several hundred engravings and drawings by Rembrandt, whose style Watelet sometimes imitated in his own engravings.[4]

Watelet began his writing career in the early 1740s with some pastoral fiction and theater pieces. His novel *Silvie* was politely received at the time, but is justly forgotten today. Better known is his didactic poem *L'Art de peindre* (*The Art of Painting*), published in 1760. Written in emulation of Boileau's *Art poétique* (1674), Watelet set out to codify in verse the principles of the art of painting. Despite withering criticism by Diderot,[5] who thought the text worthless, the work secured Watelet's inclusion among the immortals of the French Academy in November 1760. The poem established Watelet as a serious student of art theory, as indeed his future career attests. He went on to write some thirty articles related to the arts for Diderot and D'Alembert's *Encyclopédie*. At the time of his death he was writing a comprehensive and authoritative dictionary on the arts, *Dictionnaire des arts de peinture, de gravure et de sculp-*

ture (*Dictionary of the Arts of Painting, Engraving, and Sculpture*). Pierre-Charles Lévesque completed the work, which subsequently became the *Dictionnaire des beaux-arts* of Panckoucke's important *Encyclopédie méthodique*. Taken as a whole, Watelet's written corpus constitutes a major project, though left incomplete, on the aesthetics of taste in the eighteenth century.

Background to the *Essay on Gardens*

To better appreciate Watelet's *Essay on Gardens*, a brief accounting of events leading to its publication and immediate aftermath is in order. There is no need to rehearse the development of the English gardening tradition, hereafter called the natural or picturesque in accordance with French preference.[6] By the mid-eighteenth century on both sides of the English Channel the regularized French garden of the Le Nôtre style had yielded to a contrived irregular, indeed natural, garden typology. In fits and starts, beginning with William Kent's deliberate designs for Chiswick, dating from the 1730s, the picturesque garden began to transform the landscape of Europe. Within a generation or so, garden designers had exposure to the methods of implementing picturesque gardens, but a synthetic theory of the practice was wanting. That is to say, though the new gardening tradition was well established at mid-century, it still lacked an overall theoretical treatment in text. Important gardening books such as Antoine-Joseph Dézallier d'Argenville's *La Théorie et la pratique du jardinage* (*The Theory and Practice of Gardening*, 1709, with multiple, expanded editions following); Stephen Switzer's *Ichnographia, or The Nobleman, Gentleman, and Gardener's Recreation* (1715, with multiple editions following), and Jacques-François Blondel's *Architecture françoise* (four volumes, 1752–1756) may have foreshadowed the turn of events to come in the garden, yet they were not by any measure a set of works that constituted a theoretical formulation of the new picturesque art form. All this changed dramatically in the 1770s. In that seminal decade an unprecedented number of texts on the new taste in gardening were published in England, France, and Germany.

The first book that can rightfully claim to be a theoretical treatment of picturesque gardening is Thomas Whately's *Observations on Modern Gardening* of 1770. The book's second edition appeared within months of the first, a third edition followed in 1771, and a fourth in 1777. It was quickly translated into both French and German in 1771. François de Paule Latapie provided the French translation, *L'Art de former les jardins modernes ou l'art des jardins anglais*, to which he added a lengthy and important introduction. The German translation, *Betrachtungen über das heutige Gartenwesen durch Beyspiele erläutert,* was by Johann Ernst Zeiher. The frenzied publication history, and French and German translations, of Whately's *Observations* are highly suggestive of the popularity of the gardening style the book professed.

Presenting a different, yet still picturesque, theoretical argument was William Chambers's *Dissertation on Oriental Gardening,* published in English and French in 1772, with a second, revised edition in the following year. It, too, was translated into German in 1775. As early as 1757, Chambers had anticipated changing attitudes in his *Design of Chinese Buildings, Furniture, Dresses, Machines and Utensiles . . .* of 1757, which included an essay on Chinese gardens. This work was also published simultaneously in French.

Challenged by the English, the French soon produced their own works on the aims and methods of the picturesque. Though they were slow to begin publishing by the decade's end the French had outpaced the English, producing several important works. Watelet's *Essai sur les jardins* of 1774 was the first French contribution to the theoretical debate and was given a German translation in 1776. It was followed in quick succession by Antoine-Nicolas Duchesne's *Considérations sur le jardinage (Considerations on Gardening)* and *Sur la formation des jardins (On the Formation of Gardens),* both of 1775 (the latter given a second edition in 1779); Jean-Marie Morel's *Théorie des jardins (Theory of Gardens)* of 1776 (enlarged, second edition in 1802), and René de Girardin's *De la composition des paysages* in 1777 (second edition in 1793). Girardin's work was translated into English in 1783 by D. Malthus as *An Essay on Landscape,* the only French treatise to be so. Less theoretical yet important was Louis Carrogis de Carmontelle's lavish folio *Jardin de Monceau (Garden of Monceau),* published in 1779. Likewise, George-Louis Le Rouge's multivolume *cahiers* on *Jardins anglo-chinois à la mode; ou, Détails des nouveaux jardins à la mode (Fashionable Anglo-Chinese Gardens, or Details about Fashionable New Gardens),* published between 1776 and 1789, was not an original work, but included several hundred plates of extant and imaginary picturesque gardens, as well as reproducing in its entirety Chambers's essay of 1757 on Chinese gardens.[7]

Germany too was caught up in the publishing fervor. The academic philosopher C. C. L. Hirschfeld published his first book on picturesque garden theory, *Anmerkungen über die Landhäuser und die Gartenkunst (Observations on Country Houses and Garden Art)* in 1773, with a second edition in 1779. A smaller version of his magnum opus, *Theorie der Gartenkunst (Theory of Garden Art),* was published in 1775 under the same name, with a second edition in 1777, while the full, five-volume treatment of his garden theory appeared simultaneously in German and French from 1779 to 1785.[8]

These are only the more prominent books published. Others were written, but remained in manuscript, such as François-Henri, duc d'Harcourt's *Traité de la décoration des dehors, des jardins et des parcs* (*Treatise on the Decoration of the Outdoors, Gardens, and Parks*), written in the mid-1770s, but published only in the early twentieth century.[9] To these works must be added the myriad didactic poems, polemics, essays, and other printed matter which all entered the debate on the new style of gardening.[10]

Notwithstanding the number of texts published in such a brief period, there was little consensus on what the garden might look like, other than it being something different from the Le Nôtre style.[11] All authors implicitly concurred that the creation of differing landscape characters was essential to the garden design and its subsequent effect on the senses. But they disagreed on the means. The degree to which "Art"—the evidence of human intervention—was apparent in the landscape composition became a focus of contention. For Whately in England and Morel in France, the elements of nature, artfully assisted by man, were sufficient. For Chambers and Carmontelle, nature alone was not enough. For them, the garden required evident artistry. The diverging aesthetics was most apparent in disagreements over presence or absence of structures, and other nonnatural elements, in the landscape—a topic Rousseau broached on a visit to England in the mid-1760s. Not surprisingly, he preferred "cottages" to "temples," thus foreshadowing a lively debate on the style of *fabriques* (architectural follies) in the picturesque garden.[12] Such debate would become central in association theory. One need only compare Brown's Blenheim to Chambers's Kew, or Morel and Girardin's Ermenonville to Carmontelle's Monceau to realize how little uniformity there was to picturesque style. In their treatment of pure landscape features, Blenheim and Ermenonville try to mask indications of human intervention, and for the most part avoid exotic structures. On the other hand, Kew, and in particular Monceau, are filled with artful and exotic contrivances.

The unprecedented number of garden theory books published in this single decade only underscores the receptive climate to the new genre, the appreciation of which made it no longer a novelty, but a received notion of an informed public.[13] In style, content, and manner of writing, these books were in new theoretical territory. Though tethered to a previous garden heritage, they assume an unmistakable, original, and wholly self-contained quality that sets them apart from previous garden literature. For the most part they contain no plans, offer no prescriptions, ignore geometry and proportions, and to all intents and purposes contain little practical information, such as plant lists, or technical guidance, such as surveying or drainage tips. Rather, these texts are heavily weighted with pure landscape description in a direct appeal to the imagination. Without exception they expand the scope of design practice beyond the utility of domestic convenience in a concerted effort to create landscapes that stir the emotions. While some previous authors, such as Dézallier d'Argenville, encouraged a look beyond the garden wall, these texts demonstratively engage a distant prospect rich in pleasure, utility, industry, and ruin.

Their common goal was to elevate landscape gardening to an independent branch of fine arts divorced from and, for some authors such as Whately, superior to landscape painting. Further, the writers of the new texts, who for the most part were not trained in the design disciplines, implicitly or explicitly recognized the distinction between architects—the traditional garden designers—and the designer of picturesque gardens, as yet unnamed. Without exception, the writers disavowed the architect's place in the creation of the new genre. Henceforth architecture theory—as codified by Blondel, for example—would no longer be the arbiter of taste in garden design. Gone were geometry and symmetry, the formal imperatives of the regular garden. Moreover, abandoning the pure and abstract geometric vocabulary of eternal and immutable forms allowed for an existential measure of temporality.[14] Doing so opened the way for the garden to be conceptualized as a human domain independent of God.[15]

Moulin Joli and the *Essay on Gardens*

Though the *Essay* made a tardy entry into the publishing history of the picturesque garden, Watelet had been practicing for decades the new garden art his book espoused. In 1750 he began to acquire three small islands in the Seine at Colombes, downstream from Paris, where he created a country retreat known as Moulin Joli—so called after an on-site working mill. The place became a de facto proving ground where the gentleman gardener could experiment with the new notions of the picturesque. Watelet probably began to improve the grounds immediately, although the construction history of Moulin Joli is not certain and its acquisition history has only recently been uncovered.[16] Of interest, while Watelet bought the property and saw to its improvements, he was not the owner of record. Rather, his mistress and her husband held legal title, though their ownership was not common knowledge at the time. Presumably, Watelet's real-estate largess speaks of his love for

Mme Le Comte, but the circumstances, or benefits, of such an arrangement have yet to be sorted out. Nevertheless, Watelet spent a fortune—his own—creating his Elysium on the Seine.[17]

Moulin Joli is reputedly the first picturesque garden in France, though its plan seems strikingly devoid of "picturesqueness." One might say that its claim to the genre is literal, as it was depicted in paintings, drawings, and engravings by artists such as François Boucher, Jean Le Prince, Jean-Claude de Saint-Non, and Hubert Robert. In virtually all images Moulin Joli suggests a rural landscape of deferred maintenance, if not calculated neglect. Nonetheless, the mixture of the water mill, row boats, fishermen, laundresses, with tender lovers, polite society, and Latin inscriptions carved into trees made Moulin Joli a corporeal landscape of the *agréable* (pleasurable) and the *utile* (useful), the pastoral ideal that pervades Watelet's *Essay*. Whatever its true appearance—it has long since been destroyed—Moulin Joli was a destination for Parisian society. Its renown was no doubt enhanced with the publication of the *Essay*, which contained a chapter-long description of the property. Moulin Joli's importance was given a royal imprimatur in the summer of 1774 with a visit by Louis XVI and his queen. Although Watelet's station could warrant hosting the monarchs, their detour was less a social call than a reconnaissance study of the garden sensation Watelet had created. Soon afterwards, Marie-Antoine began her Hameau at Versailles.

If Moulin Joli was the product of Watelet's theory *avant la lettre*, it was left for the *Essay on Gardens* to describe the thinking that occasioned it. The book was immediately recognized for its contribution to the new style of gardening, and with its publication France made a forthright entry into the debate. Watelet fashioned his theory by incorporating the intellectual and aesthetic debates of the time, and in the process set the theoretical standard of picturesque practice. All subsequent French books on the subject would use it as a basis, if not borrow from it directly. Although the *Essay* followed Whately's *Observations* and Chambers's *Dissertation*, and cannot and does not avoid the influence of these works, Watelet's book signals an independent contribution to the French treatment of picturesque theory.[18]

To be sure, the climate was fertile for its reception, but perhaps what most contributed to its success was its modest ambition. As its title states, the work is an essay, better read in one sitting than studied at length. In style, it is intensely personal, and its frequent rambles suggest a transcription of a guided tour of Moulin Joli by Watelet himself. The work pleases most when appreciated for its grace, rather than garden-

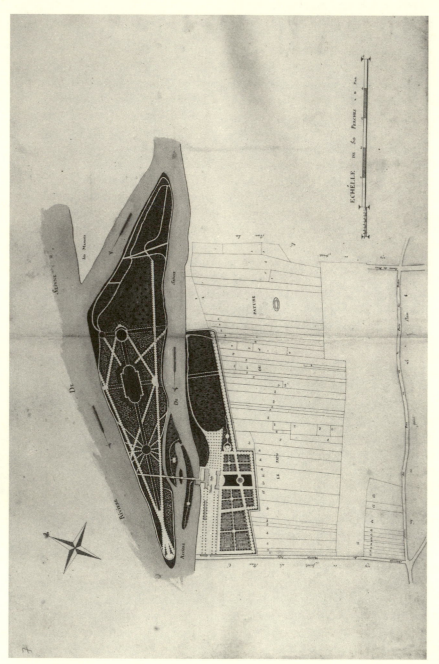

1. Moulin Joli, plan, ca. 1780. Archives Nationales, Paris.

ing prescriptions. Overall, the *Essay* sets a soothing, civil tone that res-
onates remarkably well with the society to which it is addressed.

The *Essay* was well received by the public—so much so that Watelet
planned a second edition[19]—and by the press. Though Morel objected
to the book's poor organization and lack of technical expertise,[20] and
Grimm had problems with discordant neologisms, such as *ostensive*
("ostentatious"),[21] Jean-François de La Harpe, among the most
respected literary critics of the day, wrote quite favorably in the *Mercure
de France.* "What is of interest in his style is that it seems to belong to one
of gentle manners and agreeable character, and all those who will see
the touching description of his country retreat will wish to live there
with him."[22] And the weekly *Affiches* pointedly praised the *Essay's*
refreshing didactic style and serious tone, which did not harm its
grace.[23] Hirschfeld paid Watelet the complement of including large
sections of the *Essay* in his *Theorie der Gartenkunst,* as well as freely adapting a good bit of its theory. And in a measure of how influential
Watelet's book would become—and by extension that of picturesque
theory in general—Nicolas Le Camus de Mézières dedicated his book
Le Génie de l'architecture; ou, l'Analogie de cet art avec nos sensations (*The
Genius of Architecture; or, The Analogy of that Art with Our Sensations,* 1780)
to Watelet. Le Camus praised Watelet's sensitivity, vision, and delicate
touch.[24]

To assess the *Essay* fully, we must recall that it was intended as part of
a general study of taste that Watelet left incomplete at the time of his
death. Thus, although it can be read as an autonomous work, the book
does not present a fully formulated, coherent theory. Nevertheless, it
sufficiently established the aims and methods of the French picturesque, and argued—politely, yet forcefully—for the inclusion of landscape gardening among the liberal arts. The point was not moot.
Although gardening had always been appreciated, it held a somewhat
stepchild status in the hierarchy of the fine arts. Thomas Whately took
up the gauntlet in the opening sentence of his *Observations:* "Gardening, in the perfection to which it has been lately brought in England, is
entitled to a place of considerable rank among the liberal arts." Watelet
seconded the Englishman directly—"my subject is related to the liberal
arts"—but broadens the discussion. He distinguishes between the
mechanical and liberal arts—a polarity evident throughout the book—
and reflects on the driving forces and consequences of their production. And he introduces a related polarity, that of the potential of art to
be both useful and agreeable—something ideally suited to the picturesque garden. Believing that the gardens had reached offensive
extremes of excess through artificial means (fueled by money and

industry), Watelet opines for a return to a simpler garden more in line with nature; one that relies on nature alone, rather than artful (mechanical) contrivances. As he wrote in his article on "art" in the *Encyclopédie des beaux-arts*, only the liberal arts could create sensations that satisfied the soul.[25] Thus the garden, whose metaphysical goal was spiritual satisfaction, could fulfill its duty only with a return to the *libéral.*

It is important to remember that Watelet was writing in an Enlightenment atmosphere greatly influenced by the writings of Rousseau, whom Watelet knew. In our postmodern, postindustrial world, it is hard to appreciate the importance the eighteenth century gave to art as a moral and edifying force in civilization. Such an aesthetic discourse—which dates from antiquity—is, one might say, the metanarrative of Watelet's *Essay.* The corollary argument is the corruption of the arts by the very civilization that nurtures and sustains them. The immediate source of this chain of thought was very local: Rousseau's *Discours sur les sciences et les arts* (*Discourse on the Sciences and the Arts*) of 1750, and the more important *Discours sur l'origine et les fondements de l'inégalité parmi les hommes* (*Discourse on the Origins and the Foundations of Inequality Among Men*) of 1755. In the first discourse, Rousseau warns of the corrupting effects of luxury and idleness; in the second he paints a broader canvas, calling to task civilization itself. These seminal works of Enlightenment political and social philosophy established the discourse of nature as a norm, which would sanction the claim for the moral authority, if not superiority, of rural living. Implicit in Rousseau's philosophy is the idea that a return to nature is a return to origins. Rousseau would again address these themes in his novels *Julie, ou la nouvelle Héloïse* (1761), and *Emile, ou, de l'éducation* (1762). Watelet is not as radical a thinker, but Rousseau's thought pervades the *Essay.* Watelet heeds Rousseau's message of the corrupting tendency of cities ("laboratories [of] artificial pleasures") and praises the purer virtues of country living. In his social interpretation of landscape design, the garden—as the space of mediation between nature and art—becomes for Watelet the locus of moral restitution of the human mind, body, and spirit. While the peaceful bliss of country living was in reality an impossible ideal for people obsessed with fashion, taste, and social hierarchy,[26] the decorum of a polite society transposed to the country held wide appeal.[27]

As a didactic work, the *Essay* is ostensibly about the creation of landscape garden archetypes of differing scenes. This is not at all surprising coming from an academic painter whose other written works are preoccupied with generic categories. In his *Art de peindre* of 1760, two of the four songs are devoted to picturesque and poetic compositions. In his *Dictionnaire* article on landscape painting, he distinguishes among several landscape prototypes, with a clear preference for ideal representations, as they more than any other require the most artistic genius, skill, and imagination.[28] In the *Essay*, Watelet presents a set of landscape styles—the picturesque (*pittoresque*), the poetic (*poétique*), and the romantic (*romanesque*)—to which the designer has recourse in the creation of gardens. Watelet ascribes individual characters to each category, which can be further inflected into any number of nuances through the use of the elements of nature and artistic constructions. A judicious selection of an initial genre with designed modifications and adjustments results in innumerable scenes, each with a particular effect on the senses. Moreover, a combination of generic scenes can provide for a changing tableau—not unlike scenes in a theater, to which he makes reference—and thus further heightens sensations. Though his treatment of all genres is evenhanded, he is evidently partial to a picturesque pastoral—elaborated in the last chapter, entitled "The French Garden," which is otherwise a description of Moulin Joli. With its working mill, shepherds, fisherman, and overt rusticity, the country retreat approaches a modern *ferme ornée* (embellished farm) whose combination of the agreeable with the useful is not only felicitous but morally worthy.

The chapter on Moulin Joli has a not so subtle nationalist motive. Although the chapter is intended to present a summary of the precepts and theory described in the book, and to give a virtual notion of a French picturesque garden, its title, "The French Garden," is not neutral. Consider that the penultimate chapter of the book is devoted to a description of a Chinese garden. Watelet includes the chapter as a sincere appreciation of presumed Chinese garden design (he never traveled to China and is relying on a description of others), yet in doing so he presents a recognizable challenge to England's authorship of the garden style that bears its name. Earlier in the book Watelet had already planted the doubt: "And this nation [England], it is said, borrowed the ideas for its own gardens from the Chinese." Here Watelet is participating in what was to become a long tradition of French historiography of garden design—begun by Latapie—where nationalism plays a role in designating authorship. For example, the French were quick to modify the designation "English garden" to *jardin anglo-chinois*. Appending the Sino adjective to the English garden not only deprives the English of their unique contribution, but in time the hyphenated style took on pejorative connotations, at least among the French. Thus Watelet's consecutive placement of Chinese and "French" garden descriptions may be understood as a genteel prejudicing of the former

in preference for the later. While readers can draw their own conclusions, there is no doubt of Watelet's preference and opinion: no Chinese (read English) gardens for France.[29]

A number of significant points in Watelet's treatise are worth noting
that might otherwise be subsumed in a discussion of genre. For example, though he writes "among the known arts, the one whose ideas are
most closely related to the art of gardens is that of painting," his purpose is to demonstrate their difference. In the chapter on "Modern
Parks," which is devoted to a discussion of the picturesque genre, he
pointedly distinguishes picturesque garden design as a separate artistic
enterprise, independent from its namesake art. The designer of landscape gardens, whom he refers to as a *décorateur* (decorator), may emulate picturesque compositions, but a landscape garden is inherently
different. Whereas painting accords only one view, the "person viewing
picturesque scenes in a park, on the contrary, changes their organization by changing his location." Ambulation through a garden is not
only one of its significant benefits, but essential to the notion of movement, something not possible in painting. Moreover, while moving
through a picturesque garden, the visitor is at liberty to experience it
as he or she wishes, and thus is unconstrained by the intentions of the
designer.

Watelet's conception of movement is essential to enhancing the
effects he wishes to create in the garden, but is also key to his appreciation of the dynamics of space and time in picturesque garden design.
He recognizes that the design of landscapes requires an understanding
of the simultaneous and mutual dependence of topographic variations
of "perspectives, clearings, and elevations" with the "relations and proportions between vacant and occupied space." Indeed, Watelet is the
only picturesque theorist to include a chapter on space. Furthermore,
he notes that in gardening, the vegetative cover of the earth—trees,
shrubs, grass—as well as the natural movements of wind, clouds, water,
trees, and so on, are integral to the conception. Thus Watelet combines
the dimensions of space and time to fashion a sophisticated, time-
dependent, three-dimensional theory of picturesque garden composition.

In the chapter entitled "Pleasure Gardens," Watelet continues the
important discussion of movement when distinguishing between architecture and gardening, noting the different aims and objectives of
each. His qualification that "until now" the architect was the traditional
designer of gardens is a direct challenge to architectural practice. But
the seizure of garden design from the architect is based on well-argued,
theoretical grounds. Architecture is essentially a static building prac-

tice, concerned with the immediate and stationary, and restricted to one time and one place. It requires regularity and symmetry for clarity. Picturesque gardening is the antithesis of architecture; it overcomes the inertia of architectural stasis through direct engagement in space and time. Movement is the key to the garden theory of Watelet: "Movement, that very spirit of nature, that inexhaustible source of the interest she inspires."

Watelet also engages topical aesthetic debates dealing with association theory and artistic mimesis or imitation in his discussion of the poetic and romantic garden genres. The poetic, which draws from "mythologies and . . . ancient or foreign practices and customs," and the romantic, whose actions are "more vague, more personal," require imagination and invention to set in motion an association of ideas to recall a certain time, place, climate, and story. As such, these genres draw most heavily from learning or individual experience. But they are also the genres most open to the abuse of artificial or foreign effects, such as *fabriques* (architectural follies) and other contrivances that suggest "tales of fiction and fairyland." All these devices are implicated in the theory of association, which Watelet hints at but never fully develops. Nevertheless, Watelet, more in line with the Englishman Whately than his own countryman Carmontelle, reproves emblematic devices and warns of the "errors of taste" that distort the imagination.[30]

Related to association was the theory of artistic mimesis. At issue is the degree to which Art should lord over Nature in the creation of the garden. The argument was an area of fundamental contention among the garden theorists and was not confined to national boundaries. For some, like Chambers and Carmontelle, nature was too paltry and uninteresting on its own ever to be pleasing and effective at moving the soul; nature needed improving. Whately held the opposite view. Morel agreed with Whately on the need to temper artifice in the garden, but went even further: he removed landscape gardening from the imitative arts, something seconded by the French academician Antoine Quatremère de Quincy.[31] Watelet took somewhat of a middle ground. He allowed for pastoral and rural imagery, but shunned artificiality and foreign influences, although he constructed a Chinese bridge at Moulin Joli. Such contradictions were standard fare and detract little from his essential point that "the nature of the terrain is of primary importance in determining the character of a garden scene," and that the accompanying elements of nature alone were sufficient to create a spectrum of moods necessary to arouse the soul. Though he tacitly accepts that gardening is an art of manipulation, the key to a successful picturesque garden is to balance the equation between artifice and nature. His dictum is "[come] as close as possible to artifice, while abandoning nature as little as possible," and the inevitable conclusion follows a few pages latter: "Any art that shows itself too clearly destroys the effect of Art."

It is important to note that Watelet's discussion of garden genres and aesthetic debates contains the overarching metaphysical argument of the *Essay*, and indeed of all picturesque garden theory: the affective powers of inanimate objects, whether natural or otherwise, to stir the senses and move the soul. Thus the discussion of landscape genres is about creating landscapes of different characters, which can elicit different emotional responses from terror to delight, pain to sensual pleasure. Recognizing the practical and sensible wants of man, Watelet's conception of the picturesque garden appealed to both body and spirit, and in the process combined material satisfaction with spiritual enlightenment.[32]

With these precepts, Watelet is operating wholly within the realm of philosophical empiricism, which had a dramatic impact on all picturesque theory. No doubt, Watelet's education and association with Enlightenment society colored, if not instigated, his explicit acceptance of the mechanisms of empirical sensationalism. In all probability, his direct source was the Abbé Etienne Bonnot de Condillac, Locke's disciple in France. Condillac's *Traité des sensations* (*Treatise on the Sensations*, 1754), which preceded Burke's *Philosophical Enquiry into the Origins of Our Ideas of the Sublime and the Beautiful* (1757) by three years, and its French translation by a decade, was undoubtedly known to Watelet. Condillac's influence is evident in Watelet's early poem, *L'Art de peindre*, in which he explores the activation of the senses through art. Otherwise lost in a sentimental verse—"the artist must paint with his soul"—Watelet includes unmistakable sensationalist tropes. For example, in Song Four he recalls human passions of pleasure and pain, love and hate—the binary toggle switches Condillac uses to bring his famous statue to life:

What the senses, when aroused, contribute to the passions,
The soul returns to the senses by the way it expresses them.
Joy and sadness, pleasure and pain,
Excite every nerve, flow through every vein.
Desire and love, hatred and anger,
Each has its own traits, its look, its gestures, and its colors.[33]

Watelet introduces such sensationalist writing into his *Essay* almost from the start: "we wish not only that both the materials of artistic creations and their uses bring pleasure to the senses, but also that the mind and soul in turn be touched and stirred by their appeal." Although he does not call attention to the empiricist heritage, it is safe to say that the society to which his *Essay* is addressed was well informed on the sources of his metaphysical inspiration. The importance of this heritage should not be underestimated or overlooked, as it greatly influenced subsequent picturesque garden theory and, perhaps more important, provided the theoretical means for designing gardens independent of previous practice. It is no exaggeration to say that with Watelet's sensationalist based picturesque garden theory, gardening in France had entered a new era.

Watelet concludes his *Essay on Gardens* with a "letter to a friend." It is a charming description of a garden he knows intimately—Moulin Joli. It is artfully rendered with a delicateness and refinement so befitting the era. He paints a gentle picture—more watercolor than oil—of a setting for a civil and hospitable society lived in rural bliss. Yet there is something disquieting, if not sad, in Watelet's nostalgic description of his beloved island retreat. The site seems a passive landscape, one long neglected. Three river islands made of mud and earth, with no stone quays, no harsh or hard-edged embankments. The bridges are wood and wobbly, the footpaths earthen. The air is fresh and cool. Muted birdsong, gentle murmurs of a languid Seine, Boucher-toned milk-maids, wood nymphs, and a population of real and imaginary citizens inhabit this paradise. But the season is late. The river is low. The trees are old and full, the air at midday heavy. There is a spent quality to the landscape signaled by an eroding dike.

   It is indeed ironic that at the time Watelet was putting the finishing touches to his garden essay he was facing bankruptcy. Worse, his health was failing. A little over a decade later he would be dead, and the Revolution would come and wipe out the society so dear to him. As for his Moulin Joli, what the Revolution did not destroy, time and commerce did. By the early nineteenth century, the island retreat was all but gone, its trees sold, its structures abandoned and in ruin, its contours washed away.

Oh, do not dismiss the worth of time,
For while the water rushes forth,
The wheel must meet its rapid beat.
So your days keep spinning on.
Enjoy, enjoy your allotted time.[34]

Essay on Gardens

Fortunatus et ille, deos qui novit agrestis.
(*But happy, too, is he who knows the rural gods.*)

Virgil, *Georgics,* book 2, line 493

Foreword

Society today shows greater interest than ever before in the intelligent enjoyment of the agreeable arts.[1] This leads them to multiply and divide into an infinity of branches, and to show steady advancement. As a result, the "mechanical"[2] aspect of these arts has progressed almost as much as it can, driven by wealth, imitation, and industry. We now seem to require, however, that the "liberal" side also contribute to the agreeable arts all the attention they deserve. In other words, we wish not only that both the materials of artistic creations and their uses bring pleasure to the senses, but also that the mind and the soul in turn be touched and stirred by their appeal. That is the natural progress followed by an alert mind when its desires are stimulated, and also by the soul which, if active, strives to grow and flourish.

I shall not on this occasion examine such questions as whether this general activity, greater in our country than it would be in societies less populous and less filled with idle men, is more harmful to our national glory than it is beneficial; nor shall I attempt to determine whether these branches of secondary arts, which we are so eager to multiply by grafting them, so to speak, onto one another, rob the more fundamental arts of part of their substance. Such general questions are surely interesting, but this is perhaps not the right moment to discuss them, and we should appear quite harsh if we resolved them at this time to the detriment of a great number of people among us who are almost exclusively concerned with their personal satisfaction.

I am more indulgent than that and only wish at this time to pass along a few observations I made while I was landscaping my garden, in order to assist those who find pleasure in embellishing theirs.[3] If these remarks turn out not to be disappointing, they will perhaps be followed by a more extensive collection that will consider the different arts in relation to one another from simple and elementary points of view. But in order to please some friends who are interested in the subject, I first offer this essay on gardens.[4]

In ancient times garlands were offered to benevolent divinities. This small book, in which flowers abound, is a garland I present to friendship.

To you, my friends, whom friendship guides and attracts to this pleasant retreat[5] where together we may taste those pleasures so dear to gentle and sensitive souls; to you, who come here occasionally to find the solitary peace so favorable to literature and the arts, the consolation of wise men; and, finally, to you, who, although born in palaces where hereditary virtues are preserved, do not disdain the huts where such virtues are honored, it is to you that I present this tribute. The offering is quite small, but the simple and true feeling that accompanies it may at least prove worthy of you.

On Gardens

If, under the influence of their passions, men forsake the gentle pleasures of a tranquil existence, they also come to yearn, through an irresistible urge, for the peace and quiet that they have sacrificed. A need often awakens in their troubled souls to escape the painful commotion that increasingly marks all societies. Especially when the season of nature's renewal returns, everything urges them to enjoy the gifts they are offered. That is when, lured outside the walls that enclose them, they scatter like escaped prisoners into wide and airy spaces. They can be seen wandering outside cities or climbing hillsides in search of air purer than they have breathed until now. Those most oppressed by their labors, those most chained to the yoke of their passions, rid themselves of their fetters or, if they are too weak and the effort is too great, drag their tether behind them while briefly forgetting its weight. Thus they obey nature's command, for she smiles at them encouragingly and says:

"Come! Escape the turmoil that exhausts you; escape those impulsive passions that tire your soul, the whirlwind whose thick vapors wear you down. Come, come and breathe, come and receive the warm caress of that lovely star that restores your right to equality, since it casts its light and warmth not only on the powerful and rich, but on the weak and poor as well. Listen to my voice: Build yourselves retreats where, surrounded by your children, your wives, and some true friends, you may taste, at least for a while, the pleasures that I have in store for you."

At the call of that soothing and persuasive voice, most city dwellers run off to find delight in the calm of the countryside. They build houses, endeavor to make them enjoyable, and seek peaceful tasks and pleasures in the care they bestow on them. Although their desires are still vague and their ideas unclear, their need for such pleasures is genuine. And since there is no man who has not entertained some fantasy stemming from his desires, there is no one, especially in the spring, who has not conceived the project of a country retreat. It is one of those "novels" every man composes for himself, just like the "novel" of his loves, his ambitions, or his fortune.

One should, no doubt, expect to find in these creative endeavors the same diversity that nature bestows on the individuals who undertake them. But while nature is careful to make each person different, the irresistible urge to imitate makes men resemble one another when they live side by side.

Imitation, subjecting everything to its power, imposes laws on trees, flowers, water, greenery. Most of the designs of our gardens, the shapes of our flower beds, the layouts of our groves, the ornaments we use, are borrowed or copied from one another.

There are, however, certain basic relations that exist between all these manifestations and man's needs, abilities, and inclinations. And there are also those that arise from the progress of knowledge and from the influence the various arts exert on one another.

In order to explain these relations, I shall distinguish between utilitarian establishments and pleasure gardens.

As for city gardens, their layouts seem to me to belong more particularly to architecture than to the other arts. Indeed, public walks, even most of those that belong to royal households or to our princes and are accessible to everyone, must be regarded as places where people meet or congregate. Simplicity and symmetry suit them well, for in our country, order and custom demand that everything in them be readily accessible to the eye.

Utilitarian Establishments

Rural establishments, those that conform to the original intentions of nature, are also the oldest and the least susceptible to the inevitable changes that take place within societies.

People who live in the midst of fields either resist the whims of fashion or are ignorant of them. Changes in mores and the weight of public opinion have greater difficulty reaching them; the arts and social customs are slower to exert their influence. The purpose of such establishments is usefulness, often limited to strict necessity. Considered from this point of view, they would seem to be related only to the mechanical arts, but there is always a subtle element of pleasure that enters into the utilitarian, because relaxation is as indispensable to man as work, and pleasure is one of his needs.

It is in this respect that my subject is related to the liberal arts. But let us examine for a moment the process that leads to this affinity.

When industry or power have produced in societies inequalities in skills and resources, then disparities arise in the ownership of the countryside, which should belong to everyone. Powerful and rich lords, who own large portions of the common heritage, derive a double advantage from their possessions: luxury and leisure. Yet while profiting from these benefits, they do not completely abandon the impulses that had produced them; indeed, those impulses fill their leisure time. Thus hunting sometimes appeals to belligerent peoples who, in times of peace, find it an enjoyable substitute for war. But aggressive activities do not lead to the transformation of wilderness into farmland or of the countryside into gardens. Such interests are primarily reserved for the farmers who cultivate the land. Open to new ideas, engaged by their work, prompted by their very activities toward the need for relaxation, everything draws them to the pleasures of repose, to the charms of idle enjoyments, and finally to more refined gratifications.

We shall see how, in large and flourishing societies, imitation and vanity are added to these impulses. But let us pursue our argument.

Having become less active because need—both useful and dire to men—no longer determines their behavior, landowners who enjoy in peace both luxury and leisure bring closer to their homes what they had earlier sought far away. Forest shade seems now too distant, and water flowing in out-of-the-way caves is now too hard to draw at its source; in other words, they require that the ready availability of goods obviate need, and the immediacy of gratification anticipate desire.

And so, frustrated in his idleness, man demands that surrounding objects stir feelings in him too often absent from his empty and weary soul. And as his soul has become difficult to please in the choice of sensations, like a sick person in the choice of foods offered him, he carries his desires to the level of sensual experience, whose delicacy requires the most perfect balance of external objects, the senses, and state of mind.

In order to attain such a refined degree of pleasure, man makes subtle distinctions in the embellishment of those sites he enjoys visiting. He prepares comfortable resting places and seeks out attractive views. He demands an ever thicker shade from the foliage of trees intertwined and transformed into bowers, while he requires that apart from their usefulness these trees be also prized for their shapes, their selection, and their variety. Wishing to be constantly enthralled, he gathers in a single place the flowers that had captured his attention in the fields and meadows where nature sows them at random. Moreover, he devises new ways of endowing them with perfections that nature had apparently denied them. Then, attentive to the sweet emotions of love, filial tenderness, and friendship, man discovers in these feelings even greater charms. He abandons himself to them in solitary places where his sensibilities are intensified by the happiness of birds; where the rhythmic sound of cascading, rolling water prolongs a pleasing reverie; where greenery and rare, many-colored flowers invite the eye to linger, thus delighting both sight and smell without bringing too much discomfort to the soul.

These are the steps by which art succeeds at last in embellishing nature.

But the idle, ingenious, sensitive man, after adapting the riches and beauties of nature to his advantage, experiences a particular attachment to these new treasures, and in order to secure their peaceful enjoyment, he digs moats, puts up palisades, erects walls, and thus the enclosure is created. Emblematic of personality, the enclosure is a small empire built by a human being who cannot increase his power without also increasing the concerns that threaten it.

We can easily see that in its early development the art of gardens cannot advance rapidly. In order to hasten its course it is important that the idea of shared enjoyment be added to the desire for private pleasure.

But how can this idea be implemented?

Through hospitality, which is a simple feeling emanating from nature; or else through vanity, which I shall call "ostentatious," for it is an artificial sentiment, a construct of society. To humanity's shame, the first of these feelings is not the one that propels the art of gardens to its most brilliant successes.

Let us imagine the dwellings of the patriarchs.[6] Let us consider, in our own countryside, the isolated establishments of people who are still simple in their ways and limited in their wealth.

Let us finally recall the garden of Alcinoüs:[7] a four-acre orchard, surrounded by a thorny hedge. Free-growing fruit trees charmed onlookers with the abundance and beauty of their fruit, with their selection and variety. In the arrangement of the trees was the only evidence of the sovereign's art.

A kitchen garden, cultivated with care, offered, in addition, useful produce in its various sections. Two springs dispensed water, one through the garden it irrigated, the other along the walls of the residence all the way to the front, where it benefited the citizenry.

Such, Homer tells us, were the magnificent gifts with which the gods had embellished Alcinoüs's dwelling. Let us rather say that these were the respectable conditions of those no doubt happy times, conditions well adapted to the noble simplicity of heroes and hospitable princes.

But this was in the distant past. Such customs do not last long. Our arts today, dominated by luxury, no longer owe the perfection they are acquiring to hospitality. It is rather "ostentatious" vanity that stimulates their advancement and carries them to their highest successes. Powerful and enterprising magician that it is in opulent societies, vanity causes most idle and wealthy men to adopt roles without which their luxuries would be useless to them, their leisure a burden. Engaged in such role-playing, so necessary to their idleness, they strike us as magnificent and sensuous, as enthusiasts of the arts, of talents, of pleasures, and sometimes as capricious eccentrics, or servile imitators of foreign fashions and peculiarities.

Taste, sensibility, and intelligence are necessary in the performance of these roles; unfortunately, luxury, leisure, and pretension cannot generate them. These actors, however, when they go on stage, strive to impose on everything around them the style they have adopted. If this style results from ill-conceived means or disorganized ideas, it is deemed ridiculous. But if it is the product of felicitous innovations based on nature or sanctioned by convention, then it is admired by the spectators, and its success gives rise to new arts, or at least to new and evolving types of amusement and pleasure.

In order to enrich and diversify these new arts, we ordinarily turn to picturesque,[8] poetic, or romantic[9] inventions, which are related to the fictional and the imaginary. Can one possibly doubt their hold on people! However, among the ideas that imagination uses, those called pastoral are no doubt the most suitable to the embellishment of the countryside. But our notions of what was pastoral in the ancient world have become corrupted. And if those we identify today by that name descend from the ancient ones, they are to them as our city women, adorned with rich fabrics and ribbons, are to their grandmothers, who showed to advantage a modest dress trimmed only with a spray of flowers.

Let us examine, however, what embellishments modern pastoral could still bring to a rural establishment, provided that a well-controlled art were employed to organize the useful contributions of the countryside in the most satisfactory manner. Examination of such details will seem perhaps to go beyond the scope of this elementary essay, but I feel compelled to deal with them because of the interest people take in this matter. I shall, therefore, allow myself a daring supposition. I shall place near a country residence a few utilitarian establishments, attractively presented, and I shall transform, for the very sake of vanity, the proprietor of the premises into an industrious and sensitive administrator intent on taking advantage of nature both for his needs and for his pleasures.

The Embellished Farm *(La Ferme Ornée)*

The residence should be situated on the slope of a hill, from where the eye can easily encompass the buildings and enclosures that are meant to put the gifts of nature to good use.[10]

The pleasures of the countryside must be a fabric of desires stimulated without affectation, of satisfactions gratified without effort.

The residence, then, which is meant to combine the useful and the pleasurable, should be oriented so as to allow the buildings surrounding it to come into view without obstruction. Given our climate, were it to face north it would often be exposed to bitter winds. If facing west, the harsh glare of the blazing sun, whose dazzling rays strike from below the horizon, would tire and repulse the eye. But if the residence faces southeast, our inclination to contemplate the spectacle of the countryside almost never meets an obstacle, and we find ourselves gently drawn to it by the ease of its enjoyment.

Satisfied with this orientation, I now see that the hillside descends toward meadows and a meandering stream. On the opposite slope there are cultivated fields and vineyards, and on the heights beyond there are woods that are not so distant as to discourage me from wishing to visit them. At the same elevation, but further away, I see wheat fields that give me an idea of their abundance without tiring me with their vast uniformity.

After this initial survey, I look back toward the foot of the hill where I am standing, and my eyes rest on the farm.

A cluster of buildings, courtyards, and enclosures attracts my attention and excites my curiosity. As a result, I now have little interest in seeing the garden, which could only promise a tiresome uniformity.

And so I descend the hill, my imagination bent on the pastoral mode. My desire has been piqued; it must now be sustained and satisfied. In our society, however, the more cultivated taste becomes, the more refined the artifice must be. This is an enterprise in which the utilitarian and the pleasurable must be skillfully combined to serve each other without mutual harm. It is in this sense that the art I speak of is truly a liberal art. Thus the landowner, instructed in this principle and faithful to it, has appropriately laid out even the roads by which he will guide me. These pathways constitute, as it were, the outline of his "novel." The slope of the ground where I am walking has been made gentle, and the paths trace softly winding curves. They do not point in geometric lines to my intended destination, but neither are they so tortuous as to delay my journey unnecessarily. Truly! Is not this what best suits human beings? Indeed, nothing is more like the progress of our thoughts than these paths men create in the spacious countryside, for they rarely follow straight lines. Indecision is no doubt a more comfortable state for us than exactness, and more natural than precision.[11]

But already, following the sinuous and gently sloping path, I have discovered beautiful sights, then lost them from view, only to recover them with even greater pleasure. All along I am protected from the sun by trees that seem to be there by chance, or by the shelter of small hedges that surround various kinds of planted fields. Their sheer variety intrigues me, and the care given to their maintenance fascinates me. My steps slow down imperceptibly, and I am ready to interrupt my walk, the better to enjoy the sight. The shade of a stand of trees sheltering a grass bench[12] and a small fountain brings me to a stop and beckons me to a few moments' rest.

If I resolve to sit down, my eyes are drawn by an exquisite view, and I happily prolong my necessary rest. Thus a touch of artifice adds to the pleasures that arise from our needs. Yet though the intention may be clear, it must not be made too obvious. To engage without compulsion is the art of all the pleasurable arts. Therefore, in those areas meant for walks, distances and fortuitous events must determine our moments of rest, and it must appear that chance alone has dictated their arrangement and their charms.

Various reasons can be found for pausing along the way: the size and variety of certain extraordinary trees harmoniously arranged, a spring whose flowing waters promise and indeed offer coolness, a vast prospect that requires a few moments to be surveyed, a picturesque view that captures our attention, or perhaps something unexpected that suspends our steps and attracts our gaze.

Reaching the foot of the hillside, I catch sight of the farm buildings, and my interest increases as everywhere I find proof of the care that has been taken with them. I am pleased by the attention given to the construction and maintenance of the exterior walls, where stones are combined with bricks. This diversity of materials has made it possible to distinguish base from coping and thus, with only slight variation, to embellish the construction without distorting its character. Facing the main entrance are tall trees, not too symmetrically arranged but forming a semicircle, that provide welcome shade to the laborers and others who come to the farm. A few benches have been set up for those in need of rest. In the shade, a fountain fed by water from the hillside I have just left behind flows into a stone cistern whose shape and proportions delight me with their rustic appearance. Whoever has traveled to Italy knows the attraction that certain rather common objects derive from the very simplicity of their volumes and the harmonious relation among certain of their principal parts.

Not far from the fountain, there is a drinking trough formed by the overflow of water; it is conveniently placed to serve the farm animals returning from pasture or from tilling the fields and needing to quench their thirst and refresh themselves.

Now we are entering the main courtyard. It is surrounded by all the necessary buildings whose different functions are indicated above each entry, so that, merely by looking at them I feel I belong to this establishment, for I recognize at a glance its essential components.

Order and cleanliness reign here, but without the kind of refinement that disturbs and offends when it is affected and excessive. In this place the attention given to the pleasurable must not overwhelm that given to the useful. It must never be thought that expenditures for mere ornamentation absorb the assets of a place whose function is to be profitable. And yet neglect and squalor must also be avoided, for they are more harmful to our enjoyment than fastidious refinement; they repel by evoking disagreeable thoughts of abandon and avarice.

Several gates around the enclosure invite me to indulge my curiosity. Here special courtyards are reserved for workhorses and farm animals, others for storing household tools and equipment in sheds.

As I look through these courtyards, I notice outside paths where I see greenery, shrubbery, and flowers. It is a lure to draw me into various roads lined with green lawns and trees. These lanes make their way into pastures filled with animals and lead to small structures that appear to be scattered at random in this hedged enclosure. Each building, while exciting my curiosity, seems to be competing with the others in order to attract my attention and draw me forward.

The streams that irrigate the pastures intersect or follow paths opening up before me, while simple little bridges, all different in appearance, allow me to cross over. Sometimes I walk along a hedge of flowering shrubs that I did not expect to find in such a rural setting. Now I find myself sheltered by a row of willows interspersed with Lombardy poplars, a combination that offers, because of the difference in shapes, the kind of picturesque variety one must never lose sight of. Elsewhere the paths are bordered with more widely spaced trees serving to support long rows of grapevines. Their shoots grow upward by clinging to the tree branches and join together to form bowerlike garlands that please the eye while tempting the appetite with the wealth of fruit they charmingly display.

Now I come to the place reserved for everything related to dairy products. Water flows inside cowsheds that are oriented away from excessive heat and assured of the cross-ventilation essential to good health. They are not built with any pretense to grandeur, which would be contrary to their true function. They are not overly refined in appearance or in choice of building materials. Any thought of affected opulence weakens the pastoral idea that must prevail here over all others. Cleanliness and continuous care: these are the true luxuries in this section of the establishment.

Isolated granaries are within range of the barns they serve and are protected from fires. The pastures are not too distant and extend along the curves of the little river, which, as it meanders, distributes its fertile waters throughout the valley.

There is a dairy nearby shaded by dense poplars and cooled by the proximity of flowing water. It requires some further attention, for what it offers is the most delicate and pleasing product a farm can supply. Here cleanliness is indispensable, and excess can be justified. There is no offense in lavishing care on, and even enhancing, a production that nature herself contrives to make perfect. It reminds us of a youthful time, that happy state whose charming images the poets never tire recounting for our pleasure. With a delight drawn from all these natural and pastoral images one may enjoy, in this very place, a country meal composed essentially of milk and some fruit.

If the farm I imagine is expected to assemble in one place all the delightful ideas that usefulness can inspire, then it is no surprise to find not far from where milk is prepared the place where honey is produced.

Kept within an enclosure surrounded by a palisade of flowering thorn, the beehives are arranged on amphitheaters facing south, thus sheltered from the cold of the north. The whole enclosure is filled with plants and flowers that attract bees. An abundance of thyme, lavender, and marjoram, together with willows, lindens, and poplars scent the air far and wide. The luxury of perfumes and flowers has its place here, just as cleanliness belonged in the place we left a moment ago. Thus it is that sensual pleasures, lest they offend reason, must find support, or at least a pretext, in nature.

Small fruit trees are planted in the vicinity of the apiary. Their fragrant growth helps attract swarms of bees, when they escape or are chased away, and keeps them from establishing new hives elsewhere.

Shallow, peaceful streams provide needed water and, channeled into waterfalls, produce a soothing, continuous sound that is pleasing to the bees and keeps them from swarming. The whole vicinity is planted or trimmed with vegetation that enriches the honey with healthful properties and exquisite taste. The prairies all around the apiary provide sufficient nourishment. That is not all. A small building houses the workshop where the hives are constructed during the winter; also a laboratory with some containers and a few stoves, where the honey is separated from the wax; and finally, a cool place where it is stored before it is put to various uses.

In another section of this hedged enclosure rise some larger buildings. They are meant to house silkworms and everything related to them. I do not imagine these structures to be so large as to demand individually the complete attention and arduous work of the owner. The desire to grow rich requires no doubt large establishments; as a result, great profits, sometimes enormous losses, reward or dash great efforts. There exist, however, dimensions more proportionate to man's need for satisfaction. He will always find true happiness in a combination of activities, desires, and moderate periods of rest; in lesser earnings, but not acquired at a great cost; and finally in pleasures that are consecutive and habitual rather than extensive. Besides, the variety and moderation I am proposing—still adequate, of course, to preserve one's self-respect—will more effectively please people invited to enjoy them than will objects whose magnificence overwhelms and oftentimes offends them. It is not awe caused by extravagance that you should awaken in your guests. You should offer them, and ask them to share with you, luxuries that are consistent with an average fortune. Most people will enjoy them all the more freely for not finding them superior to their expectations, and you will not awaken their envy by making a display of disproportionate opulence.

But I am ready to leave this location where I have seen the preparation and careful handling of silkworms, cocoons, and skeins of yarn meant to produce handiwork most artistically informed by intelligence and industry. Drawn by the cries of various animals, I am now heading for the stables.

Here, too, is there any need for excessive display of riches and superfluous ornaments? Intelligence focuses our attention more naturally and awakens our interest with greater certainty. The stalls are spacious and arranged in such a way that I do not feel pity for the prisoners they enclose. Rare species are housed separately to ensure purity in breeding. There is shade against summer heat, shelter against harsh weather, some sand, manure, and water. Everything that assures me these useful animals are content contributes to my pleasure far more than would gilded fences, trellises overladen with ornaments, marble basins that dry up at the slightest heat, or other features that are better suited to a kind of misplaced petty grandeur than to real usefulness.

At some distance from the chicken coop, the aquatic birds occupy their own special place. Here canals or a small arm of the little river provide them with what they require together with some particular amenities they also need. Moreover, the water channeled to their roosting place is bordered with osiers, willows, and reeds that are furnished with cotes whose appearance and comfort encourage the birds to make them their nesting place.

Further away there is still another interesting site. It is a garden containing medicinal plants essential to humans and animals. They are cultivated with care, arranged by kind, and labeled in such a way that in a few words I learn their names, their classification, and their principal properties. Such evidence of concern—an outgrowth of human compassion, economic management, and the advancement of knowledge acquired in our time—leads me to envision, with some emotion, the possibility of establishing here an infirmary for ailing servants. I imagine a clean house where, together with a few domestics, reside a knowledgeable housekeeper and a man who, educated in the rudiments of medicine, is capable of administering emergency help to the whole of this small community. He runs a laboratory equipped with the basic tools indispensable for various medicinal preparations. He manages a well-stocked drug dispensary and takes care of a very selective, hence not too extensive, medical library. The place is well ventilated, spacious, and wholesome. Some country lanes lead walkers to an oratory that dominates a hill and, seen from various points of the valley below, looks like a picturesque and unusual temple of thanksgiving. A neighboring retreat in the shape of a hermitage provides a place of rest, a shelter furnished with seats, a table, and everything else necessary for a brief pause.

As the eye embraces the whole establishment and lingers over it, one remembers the sensations already received. That is when it is only natural to say, like the sage: Oh, how happy they would be, those who inhabit the countryside, if they truly knew the value of the benefits they enjoy, or could enjoy![13] They would wish to settle down forever amidst these buildings. Thus the owner of the premises had a house built near the hermitage, similar to that of Socrates. He intends to enjoy there, from time to time, a special, more contemplative kind of pleasure derived from all these pastoral scenes. Or he may share it with a friend, for although the delectation of this kind of pleasure is best experienced in total solitude, it can never be disturbed by the presence of a friend with whom we speak of the happiness we feel. We let him enter into our soul, and we say to him what we need to say to ourselves. Without selfishness we allow him to become our very person as we savor that most delicate, pure pleasure that grows when it is shared.

The house, in order to be worthy of the name I have attached to it, must be of the utmost simplicity. By living in it the proprietor becomes himself an actor in his pastoral scene. The principal amusements he has reserved for himself are a few books and a garden full of flowers. He learns from the former, or delights in them. He cultivates the latter, or takes pleasure in observing their cultivation. He thus turns his attention away from external cares and abandons his soul to the sensations received from the objects that surround him. Above all, he leaves far behind that destructive restlessness, those immoderate attachments that are more harmful to happiness and more fatal to virtue than our natural passions.

Let him make a truce with his enemies by escaping the whirlwinds of society, whose constant turmoil benumbs and intoxicates, where phantoms pass for reality, and where the daily delirium of pride, ambition, and cupidity is seen as the most natural state. A slave now freed, let him no longer carry his chains with him. Let him at least combine a few days of restful solitude with ordinary life. What results is pleasure: ever so sensual, if one knows how to savor it; useful, if one knows how to take advantage of it. What inestimable use of leisure and luxury! The vague notion we have of them is seductive, yet the constant experience of them is tiresome; we seek them so eagerly, but often find them burdensome, even when we claim to be enjoying them the most.

In such moments the proprietor of the farm is in a position to maintain order, supervise the operation, ease suffering, and help advance the common course of a content humanity, of intelligence, and of useful industry. He sees everything, he corrects, improves, embellishes, anticipates, creates. He combines personal finances with charitable concerns. He takes pleasure in his good deeds, and time flows so quickly that he has little left to spend on long walks.

Still, he has laid out some interesting trails. A footpath follows the little river and winds alongside it, leading to rustic landscapes and well-conceived resting areas, shaded and convenient, excellent places to fish. He can find there all the necessary equipment and boats to accompany the fishermen.

Other sunlit paths offer views of the different workshops we have already visited. If the owner wishes to climb the hill opposite the one he has just descended, he finds bridges and, as the ground rises, roads lined with cherry, apple, and other useful trees. These new lanes will shortly take him, through a small vineyard, to the vicinity of a forest where grassy fields are reserved for raising horses.

Here spacious enclosures separate the horses by age groups, while thoroughbred stallions are kept in stables. There is a paddock nearby where colts are exercised and prepared for service. Thus the owner finds in this place both the advantages of a utilitarian establishment and whatever he needs for prolonged outings: in other words, a few horses born on his land and some dogs trained to rid his woods and prairies of animals harmful to the countryside as well as to the safety of his establishments.

This last scene is no doubt different from all those that were informed by the pastoral mode. But it should be remembered that bucolic ideas have become distorted and, in our country, have given way to bellicose ones. Therefore, what I have just placed at the very edge of the painting I composed can now be found at the foreground of real establishments. Parks, stables, and kennels are now located close to castles, while the farms are most often far away.

I must now pass to new subjects, leave the pastoral behind, and, as I survey our parks, propose some principles according to which they could be made less monotonous than they have been until now and more interesting.

Early Parks

In general, a park is a vast enclosure surrounded by walls, planted with thick stands of trees, and divided into straight allées that go in separate but symmetrical directions; they offer, from almost any angle, roughly the same kind of view.

The feeling these places most commonly inspire is one of solemn, often sad reverie. The pleasure sought here is that of long walks, yet they give little enjoyment for they offer no particular focus of interest. The shade provides relief in hot weather, but at the price of annoying gnats that abound because of the density of the foliage, the humidity of the thickets, and the stagnant waters confined in a few canals and reflecting pools.

It seems to me that no pastoral idea was responsible for the emergence of parks. They no doubt owe their origin to feudal pride. Powerful landlords built dwellings, or rather refuges, for their safety. Since their occupations were often violent, their pastimes needed to be safeguarded, and consequently their parks were defended by walls for the same reason that their castles were by towers.

The more powerful and rich these landowners were, the more they enlarged these parks reserved for their amusements. But what amusements! The hunt, the very emblem of hostility. Finding little safety riding through their forests, they satisfied their need for entertainment in well-protected enclosures stocked with timid animals that were hardly visible, and pierced through by straight roads that were only too visible. These enclosures were, and are still today, uniform, dreary, and boring.

As a result, dissatisfied with such vast and symmetrical expanses, they feel the need to emerge from these enclosures in order to find in the countryside the randomness of nature, far more pleasing than symmetry.

The feudal landowners, having finally abandoned the ideas of force and power for more peaceful and tranquil ones, and no longer aspiring to attain the glory of the great and eternal hunters of old, begin to endow their parks with embellishments they previously lacked. They devise idle pleasures for themselves by opening up vistas and providing them with a few artificial additions. But is it enough to contrive such pleasures? Is their effect real? Should not those for whom they are intended be also disposed to welcome them, to feel them? But this rarely happens, and that is the most formidable obstacle to success with this kind of embellishment.

The parks laid out according to the new principles are designated by the name of a nation[14] that we imitate in certain uninteresting practices with an affected eagerness that is often ridiculous. And this nation, it is said, borrowed the ideas for its own gardens from the Chinese, a people too distant, too different from us, too little known not to give rise to extraordinary notions and countless fables.

What is not a fable, however, and must be true everywhere, is that men who have acquired an overabundance of wealth and dispose of too much leisure tend toward the artificial in their pleasures, because they find themselves in a state far removed from nature. We shall examine the obstacles that impede the success of such artificial ideas, and the elementary principles on which any hope of success must be based.

But let me linger for a moment on the early parks. I will say that besides being boring—as those to whom they belong and those who visit them will attest—they are also damaging to the common good because of the extensive lands they uselessly occupy. They will be abandoned eventually, but not before all resources, which I doubt exist, have been exhausted to make them interesting.

But my intention was to speak of the arts as they are practiced today, and not to reform those I consider useless.

If I had that right or, better still, the precious gift of persuasion, I would replace the most carefully ornate parks with well-cultivated surroundings producing a variety of crops. For the most artistically decorated scenes, I would substitute hamlets whose inhabitants, sharing in my happiness, profiting from my resources, relieved of their troubles, would interest sensitive souls with the picture of their real life. And I would be far more confident of the effect of these simply human scenes than of the impressions made by the frightening, sentimental, or emblematic type of garden. Industry not applied to practical matters may command a few moments of admiration, but the effect does not last long. I would therefore propose establishments in keeping with the natural character of the region, whose material rewards and prevailing harmony would attract and sustain constant interest and attention. I would choose places suitable for projects and experiments that are always compelling in the very uncertainty of their success. Were I an affluent landowner and free to act, I would, supported by my wealth, concentrate on all these ventures such sustained intelligence as would invite others to work with me, thus filling my days and gratifying my spirit. Usefulness would be the basis of my art; variety, order, and neatness would be its ornaments. Comfortable travel and pleasant surroundings would provide access to my work of art. The purpose of this natural and "sentimental" poem would be to address both the general good and the private benefit of those working with me. The result would be a happiness and pleasure that no yearning or boredom could disturb.

In the meantime, until this plan is adopted, parks will be adorned so that opulence may serve pride and vanity, while illusions will be called to the aid of these two gods of the theater. It is important, after all, to present mannered scenes to spectators not moved by nature's simplicity, and to stimulate exhausted souls with unexpected sights, as we offer spicy foods to those with worn-out palates.

Things being as they are, let us examine for a moment the principles informing the art of modern parks, and understand the various aspects of a problem which consists in coming as close as possible to artifice, while abandoning nature as little as possible.

Modern Parks

Three styles,[15] founded on traditional ideas, may be used as bases for the decoration of modern parks: the picturesque, the poetic, and the romantic.[16]

The first, as its name indicates, is related to the ideas of painting. The painter selects his subjects from nature and combines them pleasingly according to his intended purpose. The designer of a park has no doubt the same goals but is limited in his means. Considerations such as quality of soil, weather conditions, the character and inherent configurations of the terrain present difficulties and often insurmountable obstacles to his art. The canvas, in contrast, is docile and lends itself to all the compositional needs of the painter.

Another equally important difference between the two arts is that the composition of a painting always looks the same though it may be seen from different angles, for the beholder has neither the means nor the power to alter its disposition. The person viewing picturesque scenes in a park, on the contrary, changes their organization by changing his location, and may often fail to move or pause according to the intentions of the composition.

It is, therefore, more appropriate to call the designs conceived for the embellishment of new parks "theatrical scenes" rather than paintings. But scenes presuppose the presence of actors, and those I am speaking of are by their very nature deserted and static. In other words, scenes in parks are in themselves the main focus of interest, whereas in the theater, scenes are only one element of a whole, because the goal of a play is to engage and sustain the interest of the eye, the mind, and the heart simultaneously.

This difference, although we may not realize it, has a far greater influence than we may think on the effect of the scenes arranged in modern parks.

Works of art that are not animated by movement and action, or do not appreciably evoke these ideas, are of limited interest. Even the most beautiful painting of a landscape needs movement and action to engage the eye. We look for figures in a painting; we expect them to be active or to have a clear intent. The viewer of a painting wants the breeze to appear to be shaking the branches and leaves. We feel pleasure in seeing a cascading torrent, and if some unexpected disturbance in the landscape imparts an impression of the water's swiftness, then the ideas of motion and sound come to life in the imagination. This is how a static image compensates for its lack of movement.

But figures are missing from the theatrical scenes in parks, or if we come upon them it is only by chance. The air is most often calm when we enjoy the pleasure of these spectacles. The flow of water, the rustling of leaves, or the song of the birds are the only resources we have against silence and immobility. They are thus of the greatest importance—water above all—and the more movement these resources supply, the better they lighten the silence and gloom of even the most artistically composed views.

I now pass to the difficult task of making these sights appealing from all the different viewpoints from which they may be seen.

Here the designer of gardens is more like the sculptor, for the latter, in creating a single figure or a group, uses his talent to render his composition satisfying to the eye from whatever side it may be seen. But the designer of rural scenes has one advantage over the sculptor, and that is the freedom to trace his roads and determine the location of his resting places as he sees fit. He makes use of this resource, intrinsic to his art, by curving and distributing his paths intelligently. By making them sinuous he entices the spectator to back away or move closer to his composition, according to its demands. Finally, by his careful provision of resting places, he succeeds in offering the spectator the angles of vision most favorable to his creation.

Let me now pass to the materials nature provides for the construction and embellishment of such scenes. I shall first enumerate them and then point out some characteristics of each one.

This is what nature offers us: the terrain, perspectives, orientation, trees, water, space, grassy lawns, flowers, and vistas; to these could be added rocks, grottoes, and natural irregularities in the terrain.

As for the styles that result from the various combinations of these materials, they would be numerous if we had the means, as in novels and plays, to prepare viewers for the impressions we might wish to produce, or if the scenes we arranged were viewed only by perceptive eyes and subtle imaginations, or, more important, by spectators free of cares and particular interests. Such means, however, do not exist, and such spectators are rare. In general, therefore, it is safer to restrict ourselves to well-defined styles.

The noble, the rustic, the agreeable, the serious, and the sad are the most accessible garden types and the easiest to recognize and experience because nature commonly provides models of them or because they are known through descriptions and images. There are a few others, such as the magnificent, the terrifying, and the voluptuous, but these come closer to an ideal; they need outside support, and also accessories that belong exclusively to artifice and industry.

A good way to make these types of garden more accessible is to contrast them with one another. But such contrasting, which can only be done sequentially, is not always possible, and must be handled with delicate artifice or ingenious transitions. Any art that shows itself too clearly destroys the effect of Art.

I promised some basic details concerning the materials I have just enumerated, and here they are.

The Nature of the Terrain

The nature of the terrain is of primary importance in determining the character of a garden scene. If fertile, it is suitable to the noble and the agreeable styles; if less so, to the rustic, the serious, and the sad. But if it does not present variations in its perspectives and clearings,[17] it will produce only a meager impression. In garden art, the diversity of levels in the terrain compensates in part for the lack of movement, as in architecture the presence of isolated columns and the play of surfaces produce different effects with every step one takes. We allow ourselves to be deceived by such successive diversity, like a child who, when carried by the current of a river, believes that the objects it sees along the banks are moving and must be alive.

The variations in perspectives, clearings, and elevations of which I speak are either intended by nature or supplied by art. When they are natural, their utilization is not only easier, but also far more felicitous. For art often exhausts itself by vast expenses, and then its efforts retain the mark of contrivance in a certain persistent awkwardness, meanness of dimensions, or a certain overreliance on outlines and shapes.

Orientation

Orientation is very important for both enjoyment and effect.

The scenes that the sun favors with its radiance, especially during the hours when they are meant to be enjoyed, resemble paintings exposed to the light that best suits them.

The way they receive the light gives them luster and brings forth their beauty. In this instance, the designer of gardens must see with the eye of a painter. If not, he will fail to understand fully the importance of this principle.

Trees

If we refer to nature alone, we see that trees must not be planted at equal distances from one another or in straight lines, for they grow at random. They multiply either from seeds scattered by the wind or by offshoots.[18]

If they multiply by the first method, they occur without symmetry; if by the second, they form groups. To distribute them in one of these two ways is to approximate the model one must never lose sight of. This manner of presenting trees is far preferable both for effect and variety.

It is what painters enthusiastically espouse, and unless they are absolutely compelled, they never represent palisades or allées that are totally straight.

It should be stated here that the touchstone of most picturesque scenes created in gardens or parks is the feeling they inspire in artists. If a scene is worthy of nature's approval, the painter is delighted. He will want to imitate it, and if he does, his rendition will be stimulating and lovely.

The arrangement of trees, however, is subject in some ways to the circumstances and the function of the locations where they are planted. Good taste insists on certain rules; better taste is more flexible and allows for some exceptions. But whether trees are placed symmetrically or are arranged and grouped in a picturesque fashion, it is important to anticipate the effect they will produce when they have attained their average growth and height. This precaution, indispensable for the success of the desired effects, requires, furthermore, a certain experience in thinking about proportions, and also a subtlety of mind that is closely related to the rules of composition in the art of painting, since these too deal with volumes, relations, and contrasts.

It is equally important, even when using different varieties of trees and bushes, to select those that conform to the quality of the terrain. Such mindfulness contributes to the overall effect, but even more to the timeliness of the anticipated enjoyment, and it adds much to the ultimate impression one hopes to produce. Plantings that are easy to maintain, swift to grow, and lively in appearance help produce a sense of movement that, as I said earlier, is most often lacking in garden scenes. They also inspire feelings of abundance, wealth, power, and beauty.

Water

I have already said as much: water gives life to picturesque scenes. Its principal beauty is its limpidness. Its grace comes from its freedom of movement, for grace, wherever it is encountered, derives its charms from simplicity and sincerity in action and emotion. Anything awkward, complicated, strained is harmful to it or causes it to disappear. And yet, someone might ask, is it not true that we enjoy seeing the convulsive action of water escaping from rocks, its violence appearing to destroy the obstacles that oppose its course? Yes, and our pleasure comes from the image it conveys of a recovered freedom. It is the movement that charms us when a child suddenly escapes our embrace and, with ecstatic delight, regains the freedom it had momentarily lost.

Water must be granted as much free movement as possible and should be displayed from the greatest number of perspectives. It should be channeled and guided in the most pleasing fashion so as to prompt us to follow its course past the different scenes, preparing us to view them. These are, in general, the ways of making the most effective use of water.

Space

Space gives rise to discoveries and guides the eye. This is what is called "atmosphere"[19] in paintings.

If space is too vast, it distorts the proportions of objects found in the distance or on its borders. In the layout of gardens, as in architecture, there exist necessary relations and proportions between vacant and occupied space. But empty or vacant space must never show bare land. An arid expanse or one covered with sand is the most inanimate of objects and produces the most sterile of impressions, for it is removed from its natural state. Lawns, turf, mosses, water, pastures of all sorts must be used to fill up and give variety to space and vacant land. Moreover, since the gaze tires in scanning vast expanses, it needs relief and finds it in the green color of lawns and water, which is restful to the eyes.

Flowers

Flowers are usually seen assembled in one place, clustered together, and enclosed in the symmetrical compartments that form our parterres. They are subjected to this constraint in order to simplify their watering and cultivation. Their resulting abundance, however, may weaken the impression they are supposed to create, in the same way that their symmetrical arrangement conceals their natural variety.

This is not how nature assembles them. It could perhaps be argued that she scatters them too much at random. But in order to come closer to her intention and add what is sometimes lacking in her method, you should use this ornament sparingly. Beware of extravagance. By using flowers to enrich country sites, you can make them enticing to those who come upon such wealth unexpectedly.

The fastidious cultivation of flowers entails no doubt expenses and upkeep disproportionate perhaps to the pleasure they provide. I am not, however, dealing here with the economics of gardens, but with the art of embellishing them. By using an array of flowers not necessarily credited with ideal perfection and rarity, it would be possible to carpet whole meadows in an unusual manner and give the length of a stream's banks a most pleasant and cheerful appearance.

Rocks and Grottoes

Rocks and grottoes can be regarded as accessories. They are rarely encountered naturally in the places that are being enhanced. But they may sometimes be found there, and then they serve as a transition from natural to artificial objects. We must certainly make use of such means if we wish to increase the number of garden styles and introduce nuances that add variety to scenes.

Garden Styles

Among the principal types I have already enumerated, the first is the noble. It requires a vast space, majesty of scale, grandeur of dimensions, simple arrangement of surfaces, and, above all, expansive effects, to use a term borrowed from painting. Small details must be sacrificed, trivial items banished, and conspicuous refinements carefully avoided.

To this first type I will contrast the rustic, which gives more freedom to the imagination. Rock formations and grottoes may be included here. The surfaces in the terrain may present numerous irregularities; outlines may be less carefully planned, less clearly related to one another. The layout of trees, the upkeep of lawns, the movement of water do not require too much attention.

In the agreeable style, impressions experienced in quick succession and details seen from closer up become somehow the main points of interest. If the field of view is too vast, it will spoil the response one is hoping to produce. The dimensions of the noble style are grand; those of the agreeable are average. The satisfaction derived from this style must be made effortless. Some artificial objects may be included here, but with restraint, for their predominance always weakens the idea of nature.

The cheerful style is a subtle variation of the agreeable. It is characterized by movement of water, carpets of flowers, and surprises that offer a variety of views not too broad, but filled with interesting objects.

Finally, the serious style and, especially, the sad exclude most of these adornments. The sad type must be used sparingly and serve as contrast; it is suited to melancholic beings. But melancholia always results from an affliction of the soul or a dysfunction of the organism, just as sad situations are produced by imperfections and disorders in nature.

I have said that even more deliberate subtleties could be added to scenes. But then, in order to draw attention to them, we must use totally artificial means and enlist the poetic and romantic styles to come to the aid of the picturesque.

The Poetic Style

In this kind of composition, the poetic is borrowed from mythologies and from ancient or foreign practices and customs.

The Egyptian and Greek mythologies represented the whole of nature as distributed among different divinities who had their individual mores, followers, palaces, temples, rituals, and even entirely distinct functions. Today, in our educated societies, we hold very vague notions about these mythologies, but we nevertheless take pleasure in them when the arts, in one way or another, summon them to our memory.

In planning garden scenes where the poetic genre is combined with the picturesque, our aim is to tie together, with the help of the spectators' memory, some threads of those ancient ideas, and thus make us all believe that we are for a moment transported to distant times and places. But I need not enter into minute details to show how inefficient are the means employed by this kind of magic, and what obstacles, most of them insurmountable, impede their success. We will realize how disproportionate our enterprise is compared to the means at our disposal if we recognize the limits of most people's imagination, and the general imprecision and dimness of the notions we have about ancient customs and mythologies. Moreover, we should consider the difficulties and constraints we must face in attempting to overcome our ignorance of such features as the geography and agricultural products of the regions we imperfectly try to imitate. Our only resources are a few buildings, some monuments, some half-ruined sites and incidents through which we try to evoke the ideas we have in mind. And so we erect garden structures,[20] we introduce images, and etch inscriptions. But we must always make certain that the visitors we take to view such places are first taught the names of the divinities whose temples and abodes they are about to see. These names are written in large letters on friezes or pedestals, just as names are inscribed on certain portraits of people who otherwise would not be recognized.[21]

But let us agree that while these poetic accessories may add to the pleasure of fertile imaginations and educated men, a large number perceives them only as oddities. On the other hand, if these additions are imperfect, as is most often the case, if they show excessive neglect, if their proportions are inaccurate, their character not clearly defined, their dimensions paltry, then the poetic enterprise becomes childish and its ambitions ridiculous. A vulgar or badly dressed actor makes us laugh when he appears on stage under the name of a hero.

The arts composed of a fusion of different arts are most appealing in theory, but most imperfect in practice. Bewitching to the imagination, they enchant while we anticipate their effects; yet their charm almost always evaporates as soon as they are put into execution. The totality, the details, the authenticity are missing; the illusion does not hold, and the factitious becomes apparent. The greater the ambition, the more ridiculous the result. This is how a man who boasts of great exploits to come becomes an object of ironic contempt if he does not keep his word. Imagination, when deceived, takes its revenge. Exaggerated promises not kept inevitably produce a comic effect, the kind that the burlesque genre has used with great success.

The poetic scenes I have just mentioned display, far more than simply picturesque or pastoral ones, an absence of movement and action, an absence that renders them cold or causes them to produce only a slight and fleeting impression. Perfecting this genre would probably require fitting pantomimes. Thus in China, the interior of the palace, which is the setting of a veritable city within the city, is filled, we are told, with people who represent citizens from all walks of life; all the occupations, and even the vicissitudes of civic life are there. Without such pantomimes, even if they were replaced by inanimate substitutes, who would fail to see the spectacle of an abandoned city, or one on which Medusa had cast her deadly gaze?

According to this Chinese example, which shows how natural it is to add movement to garden settings, it would be necessary to have a large number of pantomimes present in order to enjoy those scenes that include temples, altars, or triumphal arches. Actors dressed in the appropriate costumes would appear to enact ceremonies, offer sacrifices, execute dances, bear offerings, or stage triumphal marches. This way the scenes would contain performers, and so the spectators would find themselves absorbed by action and movement.

For an infinity of reasons too obvious to enumerate, such perfection is clearly impossible to achieve. I have read, however, the interesting observations of a French traveler[22] who could draw on enough talent and wisdom to enjoy the spectacle of the world and then write a useful and delightful account of it. He informs us that in Germany a certain lord has pantomimes performed on his estates that match the scenes of his gardens. His vassals, his servants, his serfs, willingly or not, at the slightest signal transform themselves into triumphant Romans, Egyptians celebrating festivals, or Greeks competing in games. But what kind of Greeks, Romans, or triumphal marches are these! And what would it not take to imitate these days such extravagant pantomimes?

If I needed to offer further evidence of the difficulties involved in taking the poetic style to some level of perfection, I would refer to the ingenious remarks of a certain English artist[23] distinguished for his knowledge and talents. The gardens he describes embrace the whole of nature. They take advantage of all genres, all possible effects; they bring together all living beings. It falls, I suppose, to none but fairies to construct such gardens and care for them!

But I realize that these tales of fiction and fairyland take me naturally back to my project, and I shall continue by saying a few things about the romantic style.

The Romantic Style

The romantic style seems to offer a wider variety of interesting subjects than the poetic, of which I have just spoken. In fact, it embraces everything that has been imagined and everything that can still be invented. But for this very reason its effect is more uncertain. In the infinite possibilities of romantic inventions there are generally only a few that are widely known, whereas poetic ideas become adopted conventions and are familiar to all those who have some education. This is because poetic ideas are read in the writings of ancient authors that are used for the instruction of the young, and also because they are constantly represented by the arts.

Romantic ideas, to which most allegories should be added, do not have this advantage. They are more vague, more personal. They belong to each individual, so to speak, and for that reason they lead more directly to a disordering of the imagination and to errors of taste. For one must not lose sight of the following principle applicable to all the arts, namely, that their productions are all the more susceptible to the abuses of bad taste when they are used for personal ends and purposes. In fact, it is certain that anyone who expects a work of art to be seen and judged by others besides himself, anyone who expects to obtain general approbation, tends naturally to move closer to reason, to nature, and to that perfection that most people acknowledge.

But, returning to my subject, I will agree that certain extraordinary garden designs, even those founded on rather childish ideas, can produce a few moments of stimulating illusion.

One example might be a very wild place where torrents plunge into deep valleys, where rocks, mournful trees, and the sound of water echoing through successive caverns bring some kind of terror to the soul. A place where thick smoke is seen rising and fires surging from foundries or hidden glassworks; where the grating noise of groaning machines laboriously grinding their wheels might bring to mind the moans and screams of evil spirits. Such images of a magic wilderness, a place meant for incantations, to which still more unexpected events and suitable sounds might be added, can produce a romantic thrill so profound that pantomime itself would be unnecessary. Indeed, the stirrings of the imagination would take its place. And at nightfall, when shadows bring their distinctive sadness and illusions, it would be easy to see demons, magicians, and monsters in this wilderness.[24]

Art could make use of such scenes to contribute, through clever invention and powerful contrast, to the charms of a wholly different spectacle. Such a contrast would render no doubt more delightful a scene whose elements had been chosen and linked with sensuality in mind. Sensuality, however, is one of the traits that can be incorporated into the planning of pleasure gardens, of which I shall now speak.

Pleasure Gardens

In order to come to those establishments where the pleasurable is no longer linked to the useful, I had to leave behind the embellished farm, far more interesting no doubt to an unaffected and sensitive soul. It is with less regret that I have now abandoned the parks whose ingenious designs most often accord only imperfect pleasures. I approach capital cities, those centers of accelerated movement, those laboratories where artificial pleasures are concocted for people who have withdrawn from nature. Here one finds, more than anywhere else and in greater abundance, excess commonly ill used, leisure often wasted, passions merely imagined, infinite cravings constantly renewed, exhausted desires eagerly recalled, pretensions treated as if they were virtues or true sentiments. Unfortunately, in our society, these are the masters whom the arts, destined for nobler uses, are too often forced to obey.

Pleasure gardens, made for the sole purpose of being enjoyable, are most often imitations of one another. They are nevertheless distinguished from each other by a few features or by some subtle differences in the character and social status of those who have commissioned their design and ornamentation.

Powerful people, and those who try to emulate them, use these gardens to display a kind of splendor that both flatters their vanity and undermines their enjoyment. Most of their country houses are residences whose size and grandeur drive nature away from the very individuals who had come expecting to find her in the cheerful countryside. Such dwellings require innumerable accessories, for they become small cities inhabited by mostly useless people, and are filled by the same crowd of parasites and idlers who everywhere seek favor, wealth, or power.

There is another class[25] of men, less drawn to extravagance and more to a precious sensuality. These people require that their imagination and senses—stimulated by unusual surroundings, collections of objects, and extremes of perfection—find all the charms of voluptuous living in the places where they seek to escape society in order to abandon themselves to their predilections. But exaggerated desires cannot be satisfied; the resources of the arts, of whimsy, and even of prodigality become depleted, and so these unfortunate Sybarites[26] languish and weep in their delightful gardens.

There are, finally, certain men of moderation who occupy their leisure time embellishing places that nature has already destined to be interesting without further refinement and enjoyable without magnificence.

I shall say a few things about these different types, beginning with pleasure gardens where extravagance prevails.

The term "powerful"[27]—a term that I shall use here with reference to the image and perception generally attached to it—designates today, in almost every European society, a factitious class, sometimes oppressed though appearing independent, as often in debt as it appears opulent, more of a burden than an asset, and more impressive than happy. Ostentatious vanity is the foundation of its pantomime, a pantomime whose aim seems generally to display greater power and wealth than intelligence and virtue. Thus, I dare say, the luxuries of the so-called "powerful," hostile to good taste in general and very often to decency, propagate and sanction both the errors of the arts and the corruption of morals. Their behavior gives rise to dismal imitations that transmit this kind of vanity to all social levels. Moreover, in societies with an overabundance of leisure and wealth, vanity often shares with egotism the right to pervert both reason and the emotions. In fact, does it not follow that good taste and true propriety will also surely lose their sway over people isolated by their particular personality, as well as over those who make a spectacle of themselves just to satisfy their pride? The former sacrifice civility and the sentiments that bring human beings together for the sake of certain individual interests that set men apart. The latter find pleasure only in the display of an extravagance that corrupts and offends. I urge you to travel through Europe and observe most of these men building houses for themselves! Wealth will be spent lavishly, but the fitting proportions among the objects themselves, and even the relations between the objects and their intended uses, will often be forgotten. Whatever arts are employed will be subjected to an epidemic of fancy or to momentary whims. Let these men contrive and decorate pleasure gardens! Human ingenuity will exhaust itself trying to satisfy vague desires and carry out bizarre intentions. Good taste, which is the mainstay of the fine arts, as faithful to nature as our knights of old were to the ladies of their dreams, concerns itself only with the pleasure of honoring all of nature's beauties and with the glory of presenting them in the most favorable light. Good taste will now be forced to yield to laborious artifice that enjoys nothing but the unusual, and the "mechanical" arts will thus eventually prevail over the "liberal." And so we shall see gardens where artificial ornaments are preferred over natural embellishments. Trees will be subjected to shapes and treatments that disfigure them. They will be made to resemble, by means of ridiculous handling, those unfortunate men whose torsos and limbs are out of proportion to one another. Branches and foliage, mutilated and transformed into ceilings and walls, will be allowed to grow only under the constraint of iron tools. Planting arrangements, like the layouts of urban apartments, will reproduce halls, pavilions, and sitting rooms in the open air where the same boredom will reign as in those gilt-paneled interiors. Water will remain stagnant in round or square basins, or will be imprisoned in conduits while waiting for a few moments of freedom dependent on the whim of fountain attendants. Marble, by flaunting the image of wealth, will claim to ennoble what in nature is far above splendor, but itself will often appear in a state of deterioration quite in conflict with its pretensions to magnificence. Dreary bronze will dull the colorful carpet of flowers. There will be innumerable vases and mediocre statues mutilated or haphazardly distributed without concern for the features of the site, the proportions of the space containing them, or the volumes surrounding them. They will resemble useless and deformed servants who, like vestiges of misplaced splendor, clutter the apartments of a palace.

And yet, in some forgotten corners, nature will still attempt to reclaim her freedom. And if it happens that those trees, tormented by constant pruning and leveling, should be allowed to grow old, they will still attain, in spite of their tyrants, tall, noble, and robust proportions. Then, having managed to raise their crowns above the reach of ladders and billhooks, they will once more assume the majestic and picturesque beauty whose wonder attracts our eyes. Then broad allées will turn into superb, high-vaulted galleries. Branches, spreading freely, will reach across without hindrance, will interweave without effort, and will be rightly admired for effects no art can imitate. If, moreover, the need for admiration—something that vanity often imposes on itself—should allow the public to enter these places where silence and peaceful solitude inspire only resignation and boredom in their owners, then a crowd of actors of all ranks and all ages, variously attired, will fill these galleries and animate the scene with their lively pantomime. But should not nature alone take full credit for this spectacle, since the trees that embellish it have reclaimed their majestic appearance only by recovering their freedom, and the movement that gives it life is due solely to these actors who freely gather to perform their roles?

It is quite clear, moreover, that such scenes are particularly suited to urban public gardens, and even to those associated with the main residences of kings and princes. But it is also true that making these places accessible to the public precludes careful supervision, details of cleanliness, and the use of ornamentation that requires constant attention. Thus the farther away the gardens I am discussing are from capital cities, the closer they naturally move toward the style that best suits them. First, because nature is more respected the farther she is from the great centers of artifice, and second, because the landlords themselves, by moving away from the cities, unwittingly abandon some of their prejudices induced by pride. Since the spectators here are less numerous, the owners feel less pressure to put much effort into the scenic presentations. This is why actors perform more freely when the theater is only half full; as a result they are more natural and often better.

This is not all. The less frequented places encourage more careful attention to be paid to those refinements that the public's indifference renders futile. Therefore, it is here that the picturesque and the poetic should be applied with an intelligence commensurate with the arts that inform them.

These pleasure gardens must be vast, fertile, and not too uniform in their design. Freely flowing, abundant water is essential, together with meadows, forests, and hills.

A vast expanse surely requires much expense and constant care for its maintenance, as well as artificial means to visit it. The owners I have in mind, however, enjoy these luxuries, which come with their rank or wealth. Accordingly, garden styles realized over a large area can ensure long excursions and provide amusements for several days.

Some sites left somewhat wild and undeveloped would only give a sense of the countryside and thus prepare visitors to enjoy, by contrast, the pleasure of more artful scenes.

Nurseries designed for the most carefully chosen flowers would be adjacent to menageries of rare animals. Greenhouses—where the art of horticulture flatters vanity by doing for its sake violence to nature—might prepare one for the later pleasure of walking through forests of ancient trees, whose neglected foliage, natural paths, and random carpets of moss owed nothing to artifice.

In other places, hillsides might open broad vistas to our curiosity. Large, peaceful lakes will invite the visitor to trust their clear waters, and boats will be preferred to carriages as means of relishing the delicate charm of the changing scenery. Streams, whose meanderings encourage indolence to seek now-needed exercise, may lead to long outings on foot. The playfulness of bubbling water will be discovered in remote spots, and this water will be all the more admired for being free of the care of fountain attendants or the fragility of machines; no foul mud will reveal that it was once imprisoned in dark conduits.

If in the above details some of the embellishments found in modern parks recur and seem to blend the character of the styles I outlined earlier, it is because the new ideas used to decorate these parks are in fact comparable to those essentially suitable to vast pleasure gardens. The latter, however, admit a more obvious measure of artifice and a greater expenditure of wealth. Furthermore, considering the personality of the landowners I have in mind, greater effort must be expended here in order to provide incentives for activities that counter indolence, as well as to devise ways to combat idleness. We may proceed, therefore, only if we recognize that designers of gardens, in addition to the knowledge they must have of their art, should also have a certain understanding of social mores.

I shall now try to make more explicit the subtle differences among these various types of establishments.

In rural establishments, the utilitarian must definitely prevail over the agreeable and be the foundation of the pleasures anticipated.

In parks, the useful must reinforce the ornamental, and art must generally be subordinate to nature.

In pleasure gardens, art may claim the right to exhibit itself with less reserve.

Finally, in gardens destined to arouse more delicate and more elaborate sensations, artifice and wealth, used to produce supernatural and wondrous effects, must strive to prevail over nature.

But let me return for a moment to certain basic and simple notions. The first principle behind the layout of any promenades or gardens is the following: to combine constantly elements that arouse our curiosity and compel us to move about with elements that fix our attention and invite us to linger.

I repeat, it is by the use of the picturesque that one is most sure of fulfilling these two principal objectives.

Furthermore, among the known arts, the one whose ideas are most closely related to the art of gardens is that of painting. Architecture, however, has until now almost always been in charge of gardens, for gardens were not deemed, as they are today, worthy of a perfection associated with the "liberal" arts. It was natural that the architect, who was entrusted with the design of buildings, should also be in charge of gardens, for these were considered to be simply accessories of buildings. Besides, people recognized a seemingly well-founded relationship between the forms adopted for gardens and those used by architecture. But no attention was paid to the difference that exists between the two arts, a difference that arises from the very nature of the surfaces on which they exercise their respective skills.

The goal of the architect, as far as the liberal side of his art is concerned, is to render agreeable all the parts of a vertical plane. The designer of gardens exercises his talents in embellishing a horizontal plane. The former must satisfy as rapidly as possible and with the least apparent effort a spectator who derives his pleasure only from a rapid view. The latter is supposed to reveal the beauties of his work, one after another, to visitors who can devote whole hours to this kind of enjoyment.

Given such differences in intention, the architect will choose simple plans, symmetrical shapes, easily accessible proportions, and evenly balanced volumes, while the developer of a garden will favor designs full of mystery, dissimilar shapes, immediate visual impressions rather than underlying principles, and such surprises as resist uniformity. Architecture will seek precision in lines and neatness in detail; but the subtleties of garden art depend on a kind of charming indecisiveness and on a certain insouciance, so well suited to nature.

It must also be noted that when an artist lays out a garden in the privacy of his study, uniformity and symmetry will result. Working on a flat sheet of paper, he is inclined to render the surface of a terrain uniform, when in reality it is uneven, to divide it into lines that crisscross each other in a systematic fashion creating repeated patterns, to trace straight allées, circular sections, half-moons, or stars. What becomes of such a design when it is executed with all possible concern for uniformity and order? The spectator surveys a part, guesses the rest, and feels only a mild desire to set out and explore it. A vast building can give pleasure by the very size of its mass. And while an immense parterre or endless allées may astonish, this pleasure lasts but a few moments. One questions the purpose of walking across such great expanses when a single glance has already explored them. Should the effort be made? Not unless one is carried along by reverie or distracted by conversation, for such vast and uniform dimensions become tiresome. But even if one were to undertake this tedious task, this walk that nothing encourages him to hasten or slow down, he would no doubt be like a man who moved his legs without going anywhere.

Let us now join the painter and see what ideas related to his art must naturally prevail in his mind were he to undertake the embellishment of a garden. Nature, which is the object of his normal observations and daily study, will constantly present herself to him, enriched by her variety, embellished by her contrasts, by her potential for surprises, and by the impressions she creates. Movement, that very spirit of nature, that inexhaustible source of the interest she inspires, will constantly impel him to enliven the landscape he is designing. Unwilling to waste his time in the strict arrangement of parallel lines traced on a flat, horizontal plane, so cold and uninspiring to his imagination, he will seek out uneven terrains and such irregularities as will spark in him still more stimulating and picturesque ideas. If he happens upon such terrains, he will surely not destroy them by leveling the ground or by undertaking expensive constructions, so detrimental to the pleasure he wishes to produce. Should he come across some old trees, he will ask that they be spared; his plans will incorporate their shade to its best advantage so as not to depend entirely on the passage of time, whose course neither artifice nor expense can hasten nor man's wishes or desires slow down. A natural spring will never inspire the artist to construct a straight canal or a rectangular reflecting pool. Rather, he will find a way of shaping a brook whose coolness, soft curves, and movement will produce charming views and effects that he already anticipates using in his painting. If, however, he chooses to employ artificial embellishments, if he includes a temple, a pyramid, statues, vases, banisters, or balustrades, he will carefully consider their use. He will proportion these accessories to fit the character of his composition, the sites, the masses that accompany them, the objects that are near them, the empty space from which they will be seen, the play of light, and the resting places he will position for the greatest enjoyment. He will use nothing to excess, for he knows that in the arts a profusion of ornaments attests to lack of creative talent, as an excessive display of wealth reveals an empty soul.

If an artist is asked to decorate in a poetic and interesting fashion a section of a vast pleasure garden belonging to one of those men who, already distinguished by rank or wealth, become even more distinguished when their amusements include promoting the arts and honoring virtue and talent, he will recall the image Virgil[28] traced for us of those lovely places where heroes and sages found peace and well-deserved happiness for their good deeds, their labors, and their adversities.

The site where the artist will locate such a scene will be a large space varied in its surfaces and multiform in its contours. There will be meticulously kept lawns arranged so as to suggest most vividly a place created by supernatural forces. The very uniformity of this lovely greenery and the evenness of its hues will contribute to the mild and tranquil impression appropriate to the subject of the scene.

Groves of evergreens will crown the elevations of the terrain. Trees, grouped together and arranged so that the eye can penetrate beneath the shade of their branches, will decorate various parts of the valley. They will spread their foliage over the banks of a river which, like Lethe,[29] will flow calmly without disturbing the tranquility of this beautiful solitude. The flow need not be too lively; its rhythm should conform to a gentle and peaceful harmony. The riverbanks should be embellished with carefully chosen flowers, distributed with moderation.

There will be, in conspicuous places, statues of famous men, executed with enough skill and care to awaken the desire to contemplate them. Then, uplifting the viewer, their perfection may transport him from the idea of the image perceived to that of the hero and sage represented.[30]

Some statues of standing figures will be isolated; others will be sitting or forming groups. No attempt should be made to raise them on high pedestals where foreshortening would render their immobility too obvious. Some figures will be set on plinths, while others will recline on antique beds under open porticos and will seem to be conversing among themselves.

A few statues of heroes on horseback or on chariots might even be placed on roads. Grassy hillocks could be used to set off these compositions and display them in a picturesque fashion, while contrasts will be created by positioning them against masses of foliage and stands of trees. By its very color, the whiteness of the marble would add to the decorum of a place where one might expect to find only shadows. A few temples, a few altars consecrated to the arts, the sciences, the virtues, and the gentle emotions, would add some luster and variety to the surroundings. Inscriptions of well-chosen, short passages carved on trees, columns, and obelisks would sustain the impression inspired by the whole.[31] They would encourage a sweet melancholy, a pleasant distraction that might include noble and lofty sentiments joining memory and reality, where spiritual thoughts would reinforce the poetic, and where both would finally bring out all the interest inherent in the picturesque.

It would surely be a joy to wander through these Elysian fields[32] where, surrounded by the most famous of men, the very desire to be worthy of dwelling among them would bring one a step closer to virtue.

The creator of this scene will be careful not to include anything that might be unsuitable. There will be no mausoleum honoring a favorite dog,[33] nor a monument erected to the memory of a bird. Trellises, fine metals, brilliant colors, ceramics, and precious enamels should be reserved primarily for decorations intended to delight the senses rather than please the soul. For it is in the soul that the brilliance and scent of flowers, light tempered by foliage, the variations in the movement of water are all joined together with the elegance of forms and the choice of fine materials.

Skillfully executed latticework patterns, painted or gilt pilasters would serve as background and support for rosebushes, honeysuckle, jasmine, and other sweet-smelling shrubs. Orange trees of every kind would surround a temple where Venus could momentarily forget Paphos[34] and the pleasures of Amathus.[35] The water irrigating these groves would flow on marble and porphyry, while gold and bronze would serve to accentuate the magnificence of colors and the perfection of polished surfaces. If statues were used to decorate niches, they would represent those celebrated beauties of the past whose charms have kept their memory alive, and whose memory constantly recalls the powers of beauty.

But I realize that this change in tone and character of the pictures I have been describing has led me to the most highly refined of embell-ishments. Should I stop at this dangerous application of an art that I have considered one of the liberal arts? Besides, is it possible to submit to general principles what in fact depends only on personal prefer-ences, artificial tastes, and on whimsies that often come close to delir-ium? As I have said, it is in such thoroughly romantic retreats that art, the agent of imagination's errors, claims to master nature. Alcina's[36] gardens and Armida's[37] palace are the models it tries to imitate; Sybaris[38] is the land where it wishes to take us; it needs recourse to enchantments. Thus, in these fairylands, artifice and extravagance hold sway over those restrained perfections that would be based on nat-uralness and simplicity. These are the places where at all times and in all nations sensual indulgences have vied with one another for the lau-rels of hedonism. This is where you will find baths, tents, kiosks, and Chinese pavilions. This is where gardens sheltered behind transparent screens and heated by invisible hearths produce—under controlled temperatures—flowers, shrubs, and fruits of all seasons, even during the ice and cold of winter. In such places obstacles are overcome, diffi-culties averted, needs anticipated, and desires aroused.

All things submit to comfortable, agreeable, and sensuous uses. Grass-covered mounds will be turned into sofas and beds; small trees and flowers will be trained into festoons, wreaths, interlaced mono-grams, and garlands. Flowing waters will produce soft sounds or will set hidden mechanisms in motion whose sweet and delicate tunes will excite the birds to redouble their song. Water will replace muslin as liq-uid draperies protecting certain rooms against the heat. It will course past dinner tables to accompany the taking of dessert. It will assume the shapes of vases wherein to enclose lights that, in the calm of lovely nights, will glow with the double brilliance of two incompatible ele-ments seemingly joined together by a supernatural force.

But what so much artifice and ingenuity will not be able to create is pure pleasure untroubled by guilt, undiluted by weariness, protected from satiety—in a word, happiness, from which we are all the more removed for exerting ourselves to attain it. The moderation inherent in good taste does not frighten happiness away, for it grows in the pleas-urable exercise of the mind, in the use it makes of talent, and the charms it finds in the fine arts. But if you lead these arts astray, if you corrupt them, if you subject them to the whims of individual taste and the frenzies of passions, if you grant them too much sway over this happiness you seek, if a weary soul tells them, "make me feel, think, exist, make me end the apathy that drains me," then their power withers in their very effort to comply, and nothing can restore the natural rights that we have taken from them.

These reflections having led me back to the subject of my principles, it would be inappropriate to linger once more on the abuses I am condemning. But I cannot conclude without saying a few words about those pleasure gardens that belong to private individuals who are limited in their resources—people who, protected by their social station from excesses and illusory grandeur, devote a few moments of their leisure to constructing a retreat where friends or guests who are interested in the arts and in nature may find enjoyment.

The choice of location and the charms of the surrounding areas are crucial to these establishments. It is an important skill to be able to give the impression that the terrain occupied is continuous with the land beyond it.[39] This is how properties are made to look more spacious without cost, and thus the unavoidable expenses of large estates are averted. For the kind of establishment I am speaking of is not vast and must avoid great expenditures. Onerous and constant upkeep and the inevitable need for transportation to cover large distances are not compatible with the modest social class I have in mind. And so here you have the principles of moderation: occupy a small space; rarely abandon it for another.

In our society, one of the major obstacles to good moral order, improved taste, and comfortable pleasures is the desire of one social class to appropriate the status of another. This leads to pernicious imitations, foolish vanity, and ruinous efforts that—after destroying the relative equilibrium among social classes, the standards of wealth, and the conventions of society—produce only inner turmoil instead of real satisfactions. What result are financial problems, inadequate simulations of pleasure and happiness, and ever-present false appearances that deceive no one.

But let me return to my subject. What characterizes this kind of establishment is neatness, order, variety, free-flowing waters, foliage enhanced by a fertile soil, minor financial concerns compared to those of large estates, and pleasing arrangements of terrains. All this must be informed by a restrained and unforced art. These characteristics can be combined in an inexhaustible variety of ways, particularly if one relies on nature and if one refuses to succumb to servile imitation.

It is an impossible task to differentiate among such an infinite number of combinations. Every situation, every terrain can provide embellishments unique to itself and relative to its character. I shall limit myself here to two pictures of this kind that will offer perhaps some pleasure by their contrasts.

The first is a description by a Chinese sage[40] of the garden he took pleasure in arranging in order to enjoy there the charms of nature, the delights of study, and his conversations with a select company of friends.

The second is a letter in which a Frenchman describes to his friend a retreat intended for the same ends.

The Chinese Garden

Let others build palaces to enclose their sorrow and display their vanity. As for myself, I have created a place of solitude where I find pleasure in my leisure time and engage in conversation with my friends. A few acres of land sufficed for my undertaking.

In the middle of the property is a large study where I have assembled books[41] in which I may consult wisdom and converse with antiquity. To the south is a sitting room surrounded by water that flows down in a little stream from the western hills. It forms a deep basin and then spreads out into five branches like the claws of a leopard. Countless swans, on all sides, glide playfully on the water's surface.

From the banks of the first branch, which rushes down from waterfall to waterfall, rises a craggy rock, and its top, curved back and raised like an elephant's trunk, holds up an open pavilion intended for enjoying the cool breeze and contemplating the ruby-colored dawn as it crowns the sunrise.

A few steps away, the second branch divides into two canals that wind their way around an arcade bordered by a double terrace, where a palisade of rosebushes and pomegranate trees forms a festooned balcony. The western branch arches around toward the northern side of an isolated portico, where it creates a small island. The shores of this island are covered with sand, shells, and pebbles of various colors. One side of it is planted with evergreens; the other is embellished with a hut of thatch and reeds, similar to those of fishermen.

The remaining two branches seem at times to move close together and then to diverge as they follow the slopes of a meadow carpeted with flowers. Sometimes they overflow their banks and form small sheets of water surrounded by fresh grass; then they abandon the level of the meadow and flow downward through narrow canals, where they fall and plunge onto a labyrinth of rocks that seem to oppose their course. At this point they roar and foam, then escape in silvery waves through twists and turns as they are forced downward.

To the north of the large study there are numerous pavilions placed at random, some on elevations that surmount other heights, like a mother standing over her children, some clinging to a hillside, and others ensconced in the hill's small canyons and thus half hidden from view. The whole area is shaded by groves of dense bamboo intersected by sandy paths where sunlight cannot reach.

To the east a small plain opens up. It is divided into square and oval beds that are sheltered from the cold winds by a grove of ancient cedars and are filled with fragrant plants, medicinal herbs, flowers, and shrubs. Spring weather and pleasant breezes never abandon this delightful place. A small grove of pomegranate, lemon, and orange trees, always laden with flowers and fruit, completes the view toward the horizon and separates this charming spot from the other gardens to the south. In the middle of the plain stands a bower which you approach along a very gradual slope that coils around it several times, like the spirals of a shell, before reaching, in diminishing circles, the flat top of the hillock where the structure is situated. The edges of this slope are carpeted with grass that at intervals forms seats where you are invited to rest and consider the flower beds from various vantage points.

To the west, an allée of weeping willows leads to the banks of a wide brook that, a few steps away, cascades from the top of a rock covered with ivy and wild grasses of various colors. The surrounding areas present only a barrier of pointed rocks, strangely assembled, that rise like an amphitheater in a wild and rustic manner. At the base there is a deep grotto that slowly widens and forms a kind of irregular chamber whose vaulted ceiling rises into a dome. Light enters through a rather large opening from which hang branches of honeysuckle and wild vines. This chamber serves as shelter from the scorching heat of summer. Inside are scattered seats formed by rocks and by platforms dug into the thickness of the surrounding wall. A small fountain springs from one side and fills the hollow of a large stone whence it drips in a thin trickle to the ground. At this point, having wound its way through meandering cracks on the floor, the water collects in a reservoir prepared for bathing.

This reservoir sinks below a vaulted ceiling, bends slightly, and empties into a pond at the foot of the grotto. The pond has only one outlet through the strangely piled up rocks that enclose it. A host of rabbits lives there, and they inspire as much fear in the countless fish of the pond as they themselves are reputed to have.

How charming is this place of solitude! The vast sheet of water it displays is strewn with small reed-covered islets. The larger ones are aviaries filled with all kinds of birds. One can easily cross from one islet to another by means of large stepping stones emerging from the water, or by little stone or wooden bridges situated at random, some arched and straight, others twisting in various directions depending on the nature of the terrain. When the water lilies planted around the water's edge are in bloom, the pond seems crowned with crimson and scarlet, like the horizon of southern seas at sunset.

We must now decide whether to retrace our steps and leave this place of solitude or to cross over the chain of craggy rocks surrounding it on all sides. Nature has willed that these rocks should only be accessible from one corner of the pond, where the water seems to have worn them down so as to open a passage among the willows and rush noisily to the other side. This depression is hidden by old firs, so that the only things visible above the treetops are stones that resemble ruins or broken tree trunks.

The summit of this rampart of rocks can be reached by a narrow, steep staircase; it had to be cut through with a pickax whose traces on the stone are still visible. The pavilion at the top, which is a place to rest, is simplicity itself. Its sole and sufficient ornament is the view it affords of an immense plain where the Jiang[42] winds its way through villages and rice fields. The innumerable boats that cover this great river, the farmers scattered here and there throughout the countryside, the travelers that fill the roads, all enliven this beautiful landscape. And in the distance, the azure-colored mountains forming the horizon are restful and refreshing to the eyes.

When, amidst the books of my study, I tire of composing and writing, I jump into a boat that I row myself and go seeking the pleasures of my garden. Sometimes I come to the island reserved for fishing, where, protected from the burning sun by a large straw hat, I amuse myself by luring the fish that frolic in the water, and study our human passions by observing their readiness to be deceived. At other times, with a quiver over my shoulder and a bow in my hand, I climb to the top of the rocks and lie in wait for rabbits coming out of their burrows and run them through with my arrows. Alas, wiser than we are, they fear danger and flee. If they saw me coming, none would appear. When I wander among my flower beds, I gather the medicinal herbs that I want to keep. If I like a flower, I pluck it and enjoy its scent; if another is thirsty, I water it, and its neighbors are no worse off for it. How often has the presence of a perfectly ripe fruit reawakened my appetite when the sight of the most exquisite and overabundant dishes had spoiled it!

Picking my pomegranates by hand does not make them any better, but
I find they have better taste, and they are also preferred by my friends
to whom I send them. If I see a young bamboo that I intend to let grow,
I trim it or bend down its shoots and braid them together so as to clear
the path. Whether I am at the water's edge, deep in the woods, or on
top of a rock, everywhere I find a place to sit. I walk into a pavilion
intending to observe my storks wage war against the fish, but hardly
inside, forgetting what brought me there, I take up my qin[43] and with
it I challenge the birds all around.

The last rays of the sun sometimes find me considering in silence the
tender concerns of a swallow for its young, or the cunning tricks of a
kite attempting to capture its prey. The moon is already up, and I am
still sitting. This is an added pleasure. The whispering water, the sound
of the leaves in the breeze, the beauty of the sky, all immerse me in a
sweet reverie. The whole of nature speaks to my soul as I wander lis-
tening, and it is already past midnight before I reach my doorstep.
When sleep eludes me or when dreams awaken me, I seize the chance
to climb to the top of a hill, there to await the arrival of dawn, to see
the pearls and rubies she scatters along the path of the advancing sun.

My friends come to interrupt my solitude, to read me their works and
listen to mine. I include them in my amusements. Wine enlivens our
frugal meals, philosophy adds the spice, and while life at court arouses
sensuality, encourages calumny, forges chains, and sets up traps, we
invoke wisdom and offer it our hearts. My eyes are always turned toward
it, but alas, its rays shine on me only through a thousand clouds. Were
these to disperse, even if they were driven by a storm, this place of solitude would be for me the temple of Pleasure. What am I saying? As a
father, husband, citizen, man of letters, I have a thousand duties; my
life is not my own. Farewell, my dear garden, farewell. Love of family
and country summons me to the city. Save all your pleasures so they
may soon dissipate my new sorrows and rescue my virtue from their
assaults.

This piece was written by the famous Sima Guang,[44] one of the most
illustrious historiographers of China and one of its greatest ministers
since Confucius.

His detailed account shows that in all places and at all times wisdom
is the consolation of learned men; friendship, their greatest happiness;
study, their truest pleasure. This description, moreover, has an exotic
quality and wears a foreign costume, features that may well pique some
people's curiosity.

The depiction that follows is only that of a simple landscape modeled on a lovely natural setting. Yet those who enjoy this kind of picture may also welcome at times a faithfully drawn sketch, even one drafted by an unknown hand.

The French Garden—Letter to a Friend

There is no better way to begin the description[45] you have requested of me than with these words of Pliny the Younger: "You seem amazed that my Laurentine could give me so much pleasure; you will no longer be6surprised when you discover how lovely it is."[46]

But in satisfying your request, my friend, is it not fair that I should also please myself? I must, therefore, begin by informing you what the place where we live was like at one time, even as I tell you what it has become as a result of the care we have lavished on it.

To the west, an hour's distance from the city,[47] the river[48] irrigates lovely meadowlands as it divides into many branches and forms a number of islands shaded by thick willows and tall poplars. The banks of the winding canals offer continuous shade and greenery that is kept fresh by the coolness of the water. The eye delights in the picturesque views on all sides and in the distant expanses adorned with villages and castles. Finally, in this relatively limited space, the variety of perspectives, the irregularity of the terrain, the windings of the riverbanks, the asymmetrical disposition of the trees, slopes, islands, and of the dikes connecting them, all produce such a charming diversity that you have no desire to leave. In this small enclosure you feel sheltered, not confined, whether by a hawthorn hedge or by the banks of the various waterways.

This unusual site had long been neglected. Its potential beauty was only waiting to be revealed when, one day in spring some twenty years ago, I discovered this charming location.[49] I was crossing the river in a ferryboat on my way to the city, calmly preoccupied with thoughts of my friends and of the arts, two subjects so dear to me that, as you know, I have allowed them to dominate all others. I let my gaze wander. The grove I have just described for you attracted my eye. An eighth of a league[50] in the distance, it presented such a lovely view that I wished I could enjoy it more fully. A meadow, flowing waters, shade! Here, I told myself, far from the tiresome and sterile bustle of crowds, away from the childish and gloomy anxiety of people who search in vain for happiness while running away from it—this is where I could taste in tranquility both the delights of study and the beauties of nature.

2. *View of a Mill with Figures.* Drawing attributed to Claude-Henri Watelet. Collection Musée de l'Ile-de-France, Château de Sceaux. Photo: Lemaître, 2001.

3. Moulin Joli. Title sheet of six etchings ("Varie vedute del gentile molino") by Richard de Saint-Non after Jean-Baptiste Le Prince, 1755. Bibliothèque nationale de France, Paris.

4. Moulin Joli. *Rowboat on a River.* Etching by Richard de Saint-Non after Jean-Baptiste Le Prince, 1755. Bibliothèque nationale de France, Paris.

5. Moulin Joli. *Landscape with a Shepherdess in the Foreground.* Etching by Richard de Saint-Non after Jean-Baptiste Le Prince, 1755. Bibliothèque nationale de France, Paris.

6. Moulin Joli. *Landscape with a Family Sitting by the Water's Edge.* Etching by
Richard de Saint-Non after Jean-Baptiste Le Prince, 1755. Bibliothèque
nationale de France, Paris.

7. Moulin Joli. Etching by Richard de Saint-Non after Jean-Baptiste Le Prince,
1755. Bibliothèque nationale de France, Paris.

8. Moulin Joli. *Fishermen*. Etching by Richard de Saint-Non after Jean-Baptiste Le Prince, 1755. Bibliothèque nationale de France, Paris.

9. Moulin Joli. *Sanguine* by Hubert Robert. Musée des Beaux-Arts, Valence. Photo: Ph. Petiot.

10. *Moulin Joli at Colombes.* Ink drawing with gouache by Franz Edmund Weirotter. Collection Musée de l'Ile-de-France, Château de Sceaux. Photo: Lemaître, 1995.

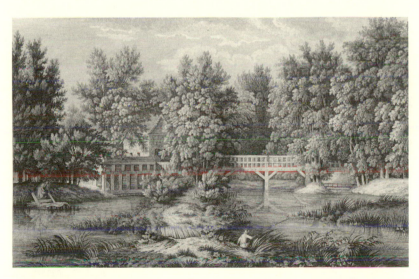

11. *Interior view of an English Garden Called Moulin Joli Near Paris Belonging to Monsieur Watelet, Controller General of Finances.* Etching in Jean Benjamin de La Borde, *Description générale et particulière de la France,* vol. 7. Mark J. Millard Architectural Collection. Photograph © Board of Trustees, National Gallery of Art, Washington, D.C.

I did not resist this first impression. Hardly had I disembarked when I proceeded toward a place that lured me by some kind of secret affinity. Walking along a narrow path through a meadow covered with flowers, I followed the riverbanks which in this location, far from being steep, descend in a gentle slope toward the water's edge. I came to a road lined with linden trees. Suddenly islands shaded by old willows appeared before me, and the sight of a small country house confirmed what I was already thinking. The dwelling that stood by the meadow resembled, in its simplicity, the vicarage of a parish priest. Near the house, a quincunx of tall poplars and lindens provided, as they still do today, a shade that the most brilliant rays of the sun cannot penetrate. And this cover continues all the way to the edge of a natural canal formed by islands and small, battered embankments against which the water breaks and bubbles as it rushes past, offering landscape painters surprises sure to catch their attention. The house, which stands on the flower-covered meadow as if on a magnificent carpet, was surrounded by a small orchard, and toward the river there were four rows of lindens, neglected but still providing abundant shade, giving the impression of a surfaced avenue that until then no one had considered using. As for the views, when I looked in a southwesterly direction, they offered me the most expansive perspective.

Here the river continues to flow for some two or three leagues alongside the plain it irrigates; then it disappears toward the tree-covered hills that form the horizon.

Along the other bank, a short distance away, is a village full of activity due to the recent passage of a ferry; still further away, other villages and hamlets embellish the scene. And this wide diversity of sights leads the eye toward even more distant mountains, crowned by an aqueduct.

Toward the south, larger towns lend even more variety to the landscape, thus revealing a vast expanse planted with all sorts of crops and fruit trees. In the distance, above this plain, rises an isolated hillock that breaks the uniformity of the various horizontal surfaces.

Facing the house, as you turn to the east, a small hillside planted with vineyards serves as background to the meadow below and reveals, thirty-six hundred feet in the distance, a very lovely natural amphitheater. On the plateau above it, you perceive the outskirts of a village embellished with several impressive houses. Their gardens, as they slope down toward the valley, lead the eye along the edge of the meadow that now appears to be surrounded solely by distant elevations, themselves dominated by even higher mountains that command the horizon.

Finally, on the other side of the waterway, there were many islands, still uncultivated at the time and independent of this small property, that made me yearn for long walks in search of other vistas similar to those I have just described.

In fact, to the north there is a small town crowned with mountains and set amid cherry and fig trees that descend to the banks of the river. The town, together with the wide expanse of ever-present water and some lovely houses surrounded by trees, forms one of the most beautiful views in this place of charming solitude.

I did not go long without taking advantage of my lucky discovery. Shortly after experiencing the enchantment of the site, I made plans to share my delight with friends, to take them to visit the location, to convey my impressions to them, and eventually become, in their company, both the owner and a resident[51] of the place.

Before long, the agreeable arts provided the dwelling with some amenities and comforts it lacked. Without disturbing its simplicity, so well suited to nature's intentions, these arts also contributed some modest embellishments to the exterior and the interior of the structure.

Out of friendship, an artist[52] famous for his masterful works of painting became my architect, just as we know of someone who once became a painter out of love.[53] Finally, those talents whose use so well reveals the value of natural beauties and the sentiments that render them so enjoyable collaborated in completing our work.[54]

Could nature possibly reject the honor of so much care lavished on her? Certainly not! Thus shade trees were planted and multiplied at will; prospects were opened at suitable places; and bridges were built. Some of these, starting among the trees, extended over islands and canals, thus providing long walks. Others, supported by small boats at water level were decorated with flowers of all seasons.[55] Roads, shaded by poplars and following the windings of the riverbanks, formed the perimeter of this pleasant retreat by linking together the bridges, the dikes, and some seemingly random footpaths. Various pavilions, located at select sites, offered necessary shelters and scenes that charm and engage the eye. Seats, cut into trees, and belvederes projecting over the water were set up everywhere. A coffee pavilion[56] was constructed under the thick shade of a few trees adjacent to the house. That is where you will find, on the bark of the tallest one, these words borrowed in part from one of our most appealing poets:[57]

Ancient poplars, pride of our groves,
Do not the haughty cedars envy.
Their fate is to panel the studies of old frauds,
Yours to shade the retreats of the joyful.[57]

A menagerie was set up near the coffee pavilion, lending, together with its usefulness, some variety and movement to the overall picture. A finger of land, carpeted with the freshest turf, was reserved for sheep that added animation to the landscape. On the avenue—formed by the bowers of tall linden trees and running all the way to the river—there was a well-stocked cow barn that supplied the adjoining, neatly embellished dairy with some of the treasures and delights offered by the countryside.

What is still left for me to do now is to acquaint you with a few details concerning our walks, and also cite some more of the inscriptions carved in picturesque spots where we often spend our time—though I fear somewhat that your exacting taste may prevail over your friendly indulgence. Some words here are well matched to the character of our sites, as lyrics are matched to charming tunes. Yet, presented out of context, they may well lose their charm and become like parodies no one sings. However, if friendship delights in details and has spurred you to imagine yourself transported to this retreat, where we wish to have you join us, then I can risk leading you to some of the places where we converse with our Hamadryads.[58]

Here an old willow stands in the middle of a shaded path that follows, almost at water level, the meandering canal. The tree appears to have seen many a generation of residents born on this shore. Its knotty bark is still topped with branches and foliage, and, at eye level, a mouthlike opening brings to mind the oracles of old that spoke, no doubt, to give men much-needed advice. They no longer speak today, but in this place they still write. And here is what this tree's Hamadryad says in an effort to persuade those who pass near her retreat:

Live but for a few friends; occupy a small space;
Do good to others, above all; have but a few aims.
Thus your days will be full, and if this joy is gone,
It will leave no guilt behind, but will go in good grace.

Quite near this old willow there is a kind of small structure projecting over the stream. It is supported by a tree rising from below, whose top branches, forming a round canopy, made it possible to construct under it a comfortable seat. You are surrounded on all sides by hanging boughs, which serve as support while allowing just enough space to sit. Nothing is more auspicious to meditation than this small retreat where the eyes, veiled, so to speak, can still peer through the foliage and see beyond. From here you can make out the movement of the water, whose sound is audible enough to induce reverie. As you rest, the boughs on both sides of your seat give the impression of moving in to let you read what is etched on their bark. One of them, uncertain of the mood of the person to whom it is speaking, expresses itself this way:

Rejoice in the secret charms
Of this delightful, shaded place.
Find some peace if you are sad;
Add to your joy if you are merry.

Another assumes a more serious tone:

Disdain renown and worldly things;
To study give your hours;
To friendship offer your days on earth—
Thus flows the time of wise men,
And worthy to be envied.
For to be loved is worth much more,
Far more than to be praised.

If while reflecting on this maxim—the heart being a better judge of it than reason—you continue on the path you have taken, you will soon see one of those bridges I mentioned earlier.

Twelve pontoons, only a few inches above the water's surface, support a one-hundred-foot-long wooden footbridge, wide enough for two people to walk abreast. Planters filled with flowers are arranged at intervals on both sides of it. The spaces between the planters are filled with lozenge-shaped trellises that allow a reassuring view of the water. This bridge, painted white and decorated with flowers, invites your visit. What you see from it changes with each step you take, and toward the middle, where it widens, it is furnished with seats. You may pause here and enjoy the pastoral landscape opening up on all sides. You breathe the scent of flowers together with the freshness of the water that you can see flowing under where your friends[59] spend pleasant evenings discussing their interests, their tastes, their travels, and where one of them carved these lines:

Behold this image of happy days!
Have we been graced by the gods?
They offer us along our way
Some cheerful sights, some rest,
And a few flowers.

But let us retrace our steps and walk to the tip of the largest island, which we have already visited in part. By crossing a stand of willows, we come, along tortuous and shaded roads, to the spot where the river forms two canals that surround this section before rejoining the riverbed.

At this farthest point we face an untamed landscape. A barren island rises in the near distance and arrests the eye. Water churns behind a broken dike that resists the current's efforts to destroy it, and, when the river level rises, a cascade forms that well suits this solitary place. The adjacent island is clear of trees that would obstruct the view; thus the gaze extends beyond it and comes to rest on a few buildings that are part of a small town not too far away. Among these structures, there is one taller than the others and therefore more imposing.[60] In itself it is not very remarkable, but who would not stop to contemplate it, upon learning that Héloïse[61] once lived there! Who, upon hearing this name, would not take a moment to talk about that frail and all-too-unhappy lover! After her tragic adventure, she withdrew to a convent where Abélard[62]—wise, troubled, demanding, and jealous—was abbot.[63] What you see here is that very convent.

If any young ladies are present when this story is told, you may expect their hearts to beat faster in their breasts, their gaze to wander distractedly; they may turn their eyes away in confusion, but then they would encounter these words which, if the climate permitted, would no doubt be carved into the bark of a myrtle:

These roofs that rise high in the air
Protect Héloïse's unhappy place.
Sigh, tender hearts, and remember my praise.
She honored Love; Love grants her life forever.

To leave this pleasant setting one may choose among many roads leading away from the stand of willows and down to the broad riverbed. Here the countryside is too open to encourage meditation and poetry. For as the gaze expands, so does the soul, which truly, but vaguely, finds delight in those beauties that distract her attention. To be inspired, the soul must be more closely contained; she must experience, without distraction and in a sweet reverie, the pleasure of familiar sensations.

I shall therefore quicken my step as I take you along a terraced road several hundred fathoms long that follows the contour of the island toward the navigable canal. This magnificent scene is enlivened by ships always sailing in from the maritime provinces. But it inspires only admiration, and it is therefore preferable to leave it behind and return once more to the interior waterways and walks, crossed by a wooden bridge of considerable span. Because of the location of the three islands that are situated below the rest of the terrain, this bridge rises as high as the treetops, whose uppermost branches provide sufficient shade to transform this passageway into a covered allée. Here you can walk without fearing the intensity of the sun, and as you move from one place to the next you can see, thanks to the gradual widening of the various canals, prospects made all the more picturesque for being observed from this rare setting. Moreover, at intervals the bridge widens above the canals, thereby making room for seats where one may rest, enjoy the coolness of the place, and delight in the lovely views.

From here one discovers in greater detail the charming meanderings of the flowing water, as well as those striking images faithfully reflected on its surface. It is only natural to speak for a moment of such beautiful effects to those who can appreciate them. This is what one may say to them:

Here the water freely glides,
Winds, and mirrors the shore's delights,
It holds its candor from its beauty;
Being a truthful mirror is its duty.

At one end of the bridge a mill comes into view. The sight of it rarely fails to attract those who have seldom seen such machinery close at hand. As you approach, you find yourself looking down at the wheel. The sound it produces, its rhythmic beat, its steady, repeated movement, all induce a few moments' reverie. You watch with growing intentness as the paddles emerge from the current one after another, slowly rising to the highest point of their orbit, only to start down again, plunge into the water, and disappear. The wheel naturally inspires contemplation, but reflections of too somber a hue would not match the colors of the scene as well as this:

Oh, do not dismiss the worth of time,
For while the water rushes forth,
The wheel must meet its rapid beat.
So your days keep spinning on.
Enjoy, enjoy your allotted time.

The struts of the bridge are supported at various points by little islands situated just above the water level. You might be tempted to descend and visit these sites; stairs lead down to them. There you would find shade and benches as well as attractive paths, though these are sometimes flooded over by the river. The old poplars that shade them bear on their boles the marks of various floods, although this has hardly stopped them from growing tall. One of them, however, more sensitive than the others to such incidents, expresses itself this way:

Within this place, many a storm
Has shaken heaven and loving hearts.
The river overflowing its banks

Covered our orchards and our flowers.
Oh, blessed gods, repair these wrongs!
To those who dwell in this modest grove
Grant the favor, under our bough,
Of shelter for a warm repose.
The lowly need but little shade!

Friendship would be sorely tried if I led you to all the spots where you could find lovely views but mediocre verses. Leisure hours inspired these lines, just as a mild spring sows flowers in our fields. But you know that flowers take no pride in being observed and take no offense in being ignored. This is also the fate of our poet-trees, and we may indeed be grateful to authors for such modesty. Do not strip them of this virtue, but decide for yourself the proper limits of your curiosity. Come join us in our Laurentine and with your presence restore what it is lacking and what nothing can replace.[64]

Notes

1. Virtually no critical work has been done on Watelet's *Essay*. Dora Wieben-son provides a comprehensive overview in her book *The Picturesque Garden in France* (Princeton: Princeton University Press, 1978). A more recent discussion appears in John Dixon Hunt, *The Picturesque Garden in Europe* (New York: Thames & Hudson, 2002), chapters 4 and 5. See also Sylvia Lavin, "Sacrifice and the Garden: Watelet's *Essai sur les jardins* and the Space of the Picturesque," *Assemblage* 28 (1996): 16–33.

2. Garden history scholarship has taken a belated, though still limited, inter-est in the French picturesque, especially in English. In addition to Wiebenson, *The Picturesque Garden in France*, recent French scholarship includes the exhibi-tion catalogues *Jardins en France, 1760–1820: Pays d'illusion, Terre d'expérience*, ed. Yves Malecot, preface by Jurgis Baltrusaitis, Caisse nationale des Monuments Historiques et des Sites (Paris, 1977); *Jardins et paysages des Hauts-de-Seine*, ed. V. Magnol-Malhache and G. Weill (Nanterre, 1982); *Le Temps des jardins*, ed. Flo-rence Collette and Denise Péricard-Méa (Conseil général de Seine-et-Marne, 1992); *Jardins en Val d'Oise*, ed. Annick Couffy (Conseil général du Val d'Oise, 1993). Ernest de Ganay's unpublished manuscripts, on deposit at the library of the Museum of Decorative Arts, Paris, are still an invaluable trove of informa-tion on picturesque gardening.

3. *Nella Venuta in Roma di Madama Le Comte, e dei Signori Watelet e Copette*. Mon-sieur Le Comte may have accompanied his wife and Watelet to Italy. The *Venuta*'s title page mentions only Watelet, Mme. Le Comte, and Abbé Copette, Watelet's former tutor. Roland—Watelet's *caissier* or bookkeeper and money manager—writes that M. Le Comte joined the traveling party, which also included servants. Charles-Nicolas Roland, *Mémoire au Roi Louis XVI, ou Journal de mes emprisonnemens à la Bastille* (London, 1784). For the *Venuta*, see Philip Hofer, *A Visit to Rome in 1764* (Cambridge, Mass.: Harvard College, 1956).

4. See Jean de Cayeux, "Watelet et Rembrandt," *Bulletin de la Société de l'His-toire de l'Art français*, Année 1965 (1966): 131–160.

5. Diderot, writing in *Correspondance littéraire*. "Nothing for the artists nor for the men of taste; no ideas, no striking precepts, no examples, nothing, nothing at all" ["rien pour les artistes ni les gens de goût, point d'idées, point de pré-cepts frappants, point d'exemples, rien, rien du tout"]. Diderot's vituperative critique was not shared by the *Mercure de France*, which ran three praiseworthy articles on the poem. Cited in Maurice Henriet, "Un Amateur d'art au XVIIIe

siècle: L'Académicien Watelet," *Gazette des Beaux-Arts* (September-October 1922): 173–194.

6. "Picturesque" is used to signify the new, natural style of garden. The term does not signal among the French an aesthetic category, midway between the Sublime and the Beautiful, as it did for the English.

7. There is no summary analysis of these texts. Wiebenson, *The Picturesque Garden in France*, covers most; as does Michel Baridon, *Les Jardins: Paysagistes—jardiniers—poètes* (Paris: Robert Laffont, 1998), and most recently Sophie Le Ménahèze, *L'Invention du jardin romantique en France, 1761–1808*, preface by Michel Baridon (Neuilly-sur-Seine: Editions Spiralinthe, 2001).

8. Hirschfeld is more encyclopedic than original. Nonetheless he contributed much to an awareness of the social needs of picturesque gardens. See Linda Parshall, "C. C. L. Hirschfeld's Concept of the Garden in the German Enlightenment," *Journal of Garden History* 13, no. 3 (1993):125–171, and C. C. L. Hirschfeld, *The Theory of Garden Art*, trans. and ed. Linda B. Parshall (Philadelphia: University of Pennsylvania Press, 2001).

9. François-Henri, duc d'Harcourt, *Traité de la décoration des dehors, des jardins et des parcs*, with an introduction by Ernest de Ganay (Paris, 1919). Ganay dates the manuscript to ca. 1775.

10. Others include the *Epitre sur la manie des jardins anglais*, by Guy de Chabanan, appearing first in the *Correspondance littéraire secrète* of January 1775, subsequently undergoing numerous editions. Also published in 1775 was the slight essay *Lettre sur les jardins anglais* by the anonymous "M[onsieur] L.L.G.D.M."; it appeared in the October issue of *Journal encyclopédique*. One might add Abbé Marc-Antoine Laugier's condemnation of the "regular" garden in his *Essai sur l'architecture* (1753), though the abbot does not entertain garden theory.

11. The style of garden characterized by Le Nôtre's designs is commonly called French formal style, although it was rarely, if ever, referred to as such in the eighteenth century.

12. See D. Malthus, introduction to and translation of R. L. Girardin, *Essay on Landscape* (London, 1783), liii–liv. Cited in Wiebenson, *The Picturesque Garden in France*, 30.

13. The era was, to put it mildly, quite astir with the theoretical debate of the picturesque genre. Many of the books—Whately, Watelet, and Morel, to name but three of the most important—were reviewed in contemporary journals such as the *Journal des Savants*, *Mercure de France*, and *Correspondance littéraire*. Although the publishing fervor reached its height in the 1770s, it did not abate.

14. Baridon, *Les Jardins*, 813–814.

15. The changed configuration of the garden with its banishment of a geometric vocabulary and attendant canon of proportional rules, and the symbolic displacement of God from the center of the garden, are part of the paradigmatic changes that occurred in intellectual history through the course of the Enlightenment. The era saw fundamental reformulations of the meaning and understanding of nature, as well as a theoretical system of aesthetics based on Lockean empiricism.

16. Henriet notes that Morel assisted Watelet at Moulin Joli, but does not give any sources. The author has not been able to substantiate Henriet's assertion. See Henriet, "Un Amateur d'art au XVIIIe siècle," 173–194. We do know that a significant amount of work was done during Watelet's visit to Italy in 1763–1764. See Roland, *Mémoire au Roi Louis XVI*. For an acquisition history see

Françoise Arquié-Bruley, "Watelet, Marguerite Le Comte et le Moulin joli d'après les Archives nationales," *Bulletin de la Société de l'Histoire de l'Art français,* Année 1998 (1999): 131–156.

17. Roland was convicted of embezzling Watelet's money, yet in his own defense he wrote that Watelet spent lavishly on both Moulin Joli and his mistress, suggesting that Watelet was responsible for his own ruin. See Roland, *Mémoire au Roi Louis XVI.*

18. For the independent development of the French picturesque, see Wiebenson, *The Picturesque Garden in France.*

19. Cf. Watelet letter to Aignan-Thomas Desfriches, ca. 1774, cited in Paul Ratouis de Limay, *Un Amateur orléanais au XVIIIe siècle. Aignan-Thomas Desfriches* (Paris: Librairie H. Champion, 1907), 173.

20. J. M. Morel, *Théorie des jardins,* 2nd ed. (Paris, 1802), cii. "This essay on gardens, dashed off by a literary artist, will, with its engaging style and with the moral values that inform it, appeal to the educated reader more than it will prove useful, with the instruction it offers, to the designer of gardens." ["Cet essai sur les jardins, échappé à la plume d'un écrivain-artiste, plaira plus au lecteur lettré, par l'agrément du style et par la morale qui y est répandue, qu'il ne sera utile à l'artiste-jardinier par les leçons qu'il renferme."]

21 Grimm, *Correspondance littéraire* (December 1774), ed. Maurice Tourneux, *Correspondance littéraire, philosophique et critique par Grimm, Diderot, Raynal, Meister, etc.,* vol. 10. (Paris: Garnier Frères, 1879).

22. La Harpe, *Mercure de France* (January 1775). "L'intérêt de son style semble appartenir à des mœurs douces et à un caractère aimable; et tous ceux qui verront la description touchante de sa retraite champêtre, désireront de l'habiter avec lui."

23. Reviews of Watelet's *Essay* appeared in *Correspondance Littéraire* (December 1774); *Mercure de France* (January 1775); *L'Esprit des journaux* (February 1775); and *Affiches, annonces, et avis divers* (March 1775).

24. See Robin Middleton, introduction to Nicolas Le Camus de Mézières, *The Genius of Architecture; or, The Analogy of that Art with our Sensations,* trans. David Britt (Santa Monica, Calif.: Getty Center for the History of Art and the Humanities, 1992).

25. C.-H. Watelet and P.-C. Lévesque, *Encyclopédie méthodique. Encyclopédie des beaux-arts* (Paris: Panckoucke, 1788), 31.

26. Cf. Horace Walpole, *Anecdotes of Painting in England* (Strawberry Hill, 1762–1771), vol. 4: 35–36 (cited in Wiebenson, *The Picturesque Garden in France,* 4).

27. Watelet found further, if not more sympathetic, support for the pleasures, rewards, and virtues of country living in the pastoral literature of the day. Of particular note is Honoré d'Urfé's early seventeenth-century novel *Astrée.* The story, which had a revival of sorts in the mid-eighteenth century, unfolds in a nostalgic, idealized rural past, a time of simple living, devoid of the stress, excess, and tensions associated with that of the society, i.e., the city. The novel found its painterly counterpart in the *fêtes galantes* of Jean-Antoine Watteau, Nicolas Lancret, and Jean-Baptiste Joseph Pater, to name but a few.

28. It is of interest that Lévesque, who completed the *Dictionnaire,* appended to Watelet's landscape painting article the entirety of Roger de Piles's chapter from *Cours de peinture* (1708) on the same theme. This is suggestive of the importance landscape painting had achieved among the genres, which for

most of the eighteenth century was subordinate to history painting. See C.-H. Watelet and Pierre-Charles Lévesque, *Dictionnaire des arts de peinture, sculpture et gravure*, 5 vols. (Paris, 1792).

29. In his introduction to Whately's *Observations*, Latapie undermined the English origins of the picturesque garden, saying that the English garden was nothing more than an imitation of Chinese gardens. Le Rouge followed Latapie's lead, as did Watelet, who pointedly added that they should not be a model for France.

30. As a garden element most under human control, structures have the most potential to effect character because of the long history of association between architectural form and ornament with meaning. Thus recourse to architectural follies, while offering the quickest means of expressing character, was most open to abuse. See Thomas Whately, *Observations on Modern Gardening* (New York: Garland, 1982), 150–151.

31. Though they agreed on removing gardening from the imitative arts, Morel and Quatremère reached dramatically different conclusions on the merits of the art of picturesque gardening. See Jean-Marie Morel, *Théorie des jardins* (Paris, 1776), 380–381; and A.-C. Quatremère de Quincy, *De L'Imitation* (Paris, 1823), 149–150.

32. See Middleton, introduction to Nicolas Le Camus de Mézières, *The Genius of Architecture*, 46–51.

33. Watelet, *L'Art de peindre*, 1760, "Song Four," 54. "Ce que les sens émus prêtent aux passions, / L'âme le rend aux sens par les expressions. / La joie et le chagrin, le plaisir et la peine, / Font mouvoir chaque nerf, coulent dans chaque veine. / Les désirs et l'amour, la haine et les fureurs, / Ont leurs traits, leurs regards, leurs gestes, leur couleurs."

34. Watelet, *L'Art de peindre*, 1760, "Song Four," 93. "Ah! connaissez le prix du tems; / Tandis que l'onde s'écoule, / Que la roue obéit à ses prompts mouvemens; / De vos beaux jours le fuseau roule. / Jouissez, jouissez, ne perdez pas d'instans."

Essay on Gardens

1. Watelet uses the expression "les arts agréables," the agreeable arts, also called the pleasurable or decorative arts, which include garden design and landscaping. "Agreeable" is what he also calls one of the garden styles he discusses.

2. Throughout the *Essay*, Watelet makes a clear distinction between the "mechanical" and the "liberal" sides of the agreeable arts. The former is the practical, applied, artificial, and manual aspect that also includes the use of science and industry; the latter is the aesthetic, artistic, theoretical, natural, and affective aspect. See the *Dictionnaire de l'Académie Française*, 1694 and 1798.

3. A German translation of *Essai sur les jardins* appeared in Leipzig in 1776, but already in 1775 C. C. L. Hirschfeld (1742–1792) had written a review of it. What follows is a paraphrase of that review. "Watelet, an artist and poet of standing, was the first of his nation to submit gardens to the rules of reason and taste in a treatise of his own. His principles arose from thoughtful reflection augmented by all the benefits of a vivid imagination. Familiar with the maxims and effects of painting, he applied the rules of that art form, as far as it is possible

to do so, to the art of gardening. This he accomplished with much greater success than previous teachers of architecture, who very improperly transformed symmetry into garden designs. Admittedly, the organization of his principles is not entirely coherent, yet it is natural enough. Recognizing that this art has not yet been elevated to a science, indeed seemed hardly mature enough for it, he perhaps found it easier just to toss out a few basic rules and related applications and thereby engage both the intellect and the sensibility of his countrymen. The contribution of his treatise is much enhanced by the animated feeling he brings to his subject and by his fine and picturesque writing style." See C. C. L. Hirschfeld, *Theory of Garden Art*, ed. and trans. Linda B. Parshall (Philadelphia: University of Pennsylvania Press, 2001), 129.

4. Le Prince de Ligne writes: "After viewing the works of M. Watelet and M. de Girardin, I almost gave up working. After reading their treatises, I almost gave up writing. How could both of them say so many new, gallant, philosophical, and sublime things? . . . The first is more of a poet and more costly to follow, the second, more of a slave to Nature. The first would subject her to the power of his imagination if there were treasures that might aid him. The second seems to prescribe a surer progress. Which of the two has more soul and spirit? . . . What I know best is that I was enchanted first by reading them both and later by asking myself what I had learned. I do not wish to enchant anyone—nor can I. But I trust my gardener will understand me." Prince Charles Joseph de Ligne, *Coup d'Œil at Belœil and a Great Number of European Gardens*, trans. and ed. Basil Guy (Berkeley: University of California Press, 1991), 190. (The other writer mentioned by Ligne is René-Louis de Girardin [1735–1808], who in 1777 published a treatise on gardens, *De la composition des paysages, ou des moyens d'embellir la nature autour des habitations, en joignant l'agréable à l'utile.* It was translated in 1783 by D. Malthus as "An Essay on Landscape; or, on the means of improving and embellishing the country around our habitations." A modern reprint was published by Garland [New York, 1982]. Girardin, owner and principal designer of the gardens at Ermenonville, was a close friend of Jean-Jacques Rousseau.)

5. Watelet's estate, Moulin Joli, near the city of Bezons, between Colombes and Argenteuil, a short distance northwest of Paris.

6. A reference to biblical figures.

7. King of Phaeacia, who welcomed Ulysses to his palace. In the following passage, Ulysses, standing outside the palace, describes Alcinoüs's orchard and garden. Homer, *The Odyssey*, trans. Robert Fitzgerald (New York: Doubleday, 1961), 7.114–139. "To the left and right, outside, he saw an orchard/ closed by a pale—four spacious acres planted/ with trees in bloom or weighted down for picking:/ pear trees, pomegranates, brilliant apples,/ luscious figs, and olives ripe and dark./ Fruit never failed upon these trees: winter/ and summer time they bore, for through the year/ the breathing Westwind ripened all in turn—/ so one pear came to prime, and then another,/ and so with apples, figs, and the vine's fruit/ empurpled in the royal vineyard there./ Currants were dried at one end, on a platform/ bare to the sun, beyond the vintage arbors/ and vats the vintners trod; while near at hand/ were new grapes barely formed as the green bloom fell,/ or half-ripe clusters, faintly coloring./ After the vines came rows of vegetables/ of all the kinds that flourish in every season,/ and through the garden plots and orchard ran/ channels from one clear fountain, while another/ gushed through a pipe under the courtyard entrance/ to serve the

house and all who came for water./ These were the gifts of heaven to Alkínoös./ Odysseus, who had borne the barren sea,/ stood in the gateway and surveyed this bounty./ He gazed his fill, then swiftly he went in."

8. See Dora Wiebenson, *The Picturesque Garden in France* (Princeton: Princeton University Press, 1978). I am indebted to Wiebenson's study for most of the references to garden history; also to Michel Baridon for his impressive anthology of texts and commentaries on garden history, *Les Jardins: Paysagistes—jardiniers—poètes* (Paris: Robert Laffont, 1998); and to Michel Conan for his very helpful *Dictionnaire historique de l'art des jardins* (Paris: Hazan, 1997).

9. The term Watelet uses is "romanesque," rendered throughout this translation by "romantic." By 1774, when the *Essay on Gardens* was published, the term "romantique," borrowed from English "romantic," was slowly being used in France to refer to both the manner of experiencing a certain literary sensibility and the landscape of gardens. (See Robert, *Dictionnaire historique de la langue française*. The example given under the entry "romantique" is taken from Watelet's use of "romanesque" in the *Essay*.) The reader should keep in mind, however, that the French term "romanesque," as used by Watelet and others, retains in part its original meaning of "fictional," i.e., having to do with characteristics of novels (*romans*). Jean-Jacques Rousseau's epistolary novel, *Julie ou la nouvelle Héloïse* (1761), contributed much to the evolution of sensibility from "romanesque" to "romantic" in the late eighteenth century; in the Fifth Walk of 1777 (*Les Rêveries du promeneur solitaire*), Rousseau uses both "romanesque" and "romantique," but employs the latter to express the sensation produced by a solitary landscape. In chapter 15 of *De la composition des paysages* (1777) entitled "The power of landscapes on our senses and as a result on our soul," René de Girardin, in a footnote, distinguishes between the two terms, "romanesque" and "romantique," as follows: "the first tends to designate the story in the novel and the second designates the state and touching impression we experience as a result of the first." (See H. Roddier's introduction and excellent essay, "Rousseau et le marquis de Girardin ou Comment l'art des jardins conduit du *romanesque* au *romantisme*" ("Rousseau and the Marquis de Girardin, or How the Art of Gardens Leads from Romanesque to Romanticism") in J. J. Rousseau, *Les Rêveries du promeneur solitaire*, ed. Roddier (Paris: Garnier, 1997).

10. C. C. L. Hirschfeld in his five-volume *Theorie der Gartenkunst* (published from 1779 to 1785), cites a large portion of this chapter, which he introduces as follows: "Some time later in France, the artist Watelet offered a lovely description of an ornamented farm (*ferme ornée*), which diverges somewhat from British ideas but which makes a light and charming composition." Hirschfeld, *Theory of Garden Art*, 424.

11. This passage and the following bring to mind, among others, Sterne's *Tristram Shandy* (1760–1767), Diderot's *Jacques le fataliste* (1778–1780, 1796), or Hogarth's "serpentine line," defined, on the artist's palette, as "The Line of Beauty" and elsewhere in *The Analysis of Beauty* (48–59) as "the line of grace."

12. A benchlike formation in the ground covered with grass.

13. Watelet quotes from Virgil's *Georgics*: "O fortunatos nimium, sua si bona norint, agricolas!" ("O farmers, happy beyond measure, could they but know their blessings!") Virgil, *Eclogues, Georgics, Aeneid 1–6*, trans. H. Rushton Fairclough, rev. G. P. Goold, Loeb Classical Library (Cambridge, Mass.: Harvard University Press, 1999), book 2, lines 458–459.

14. I.e., England.

15. Watelet uses "caractère." Although "style" is often limited to architecture,

it is used here, together with "type" and "character," to refer to the various kinds of gardens described by the author.

16. See note 9.

17. The term Watelet uses is "coupe," referring to a space in a wooded area where the trees have been cut down to be used as lumber or have been brought down by a storm.

18. See Virgil, *Georgics,* book 2, lines 9–21.

19. Watelet uses "air." When applied to a painting, "air" is a technical term referring to the space allowed between the elements contained in a composition, to their discrete edges, to clear depth differentiation, to the absence of clutter; a term that could also be used is "spaciousness." See *Dictionnaire de l'Académie Française,* 1798.

20. The expression Watelet employs is "fabrique," a technical term in landscape painting used to designate all the structures, sometimes ruins, added to enliven a landscape, such as temples to various divinities, pagodas, pyramids, porticos, towers, kiosks, gazebos, and altars. In the landscape of gardens, such buildings are often called "follies."

21. See T. Whately, *Observations on Modern Gardening* (1770); the French translation of this work appeared in 1771. Watelet no doubt knew of it, for he incorporates here some of Whately's ideas on the "emblematic character" of certain gardens. See Wiebenson, *Picturesque Garden in France,* 45. On Whately's terms, see John Dixon Hunt, "Emblem and Expression in the Eighteenth-Century Landscape Garden," in *Gardens and the Picturesque: Studies in the History of Landscape Architecture* (Cambridge, Mass.: MIT Press, 1992), 75–104.

22. He has not been identified.

23. Some believe that the "English artist" mentioned here is none other than William Chambers with whose work Watelet was no doubt familiar. See R. C. Bald, "Sir William Chambers and the Chinese Garden," *Journal of the History of Ideas,* 10, no. 3 (June 1950): 287–320. In this article, Bald cites the following passage from a letter by Chambers dated May 13, 1772, addressed to an unidentified critic (possibly Horace Walpole) of his *Treatise on Oriental Gardening:* "I would endeavour to go further, & not only improve, but adorn Nature with suitable accompanyments, not only provide for the comforts, but for the most exalted pleasures of life; far from being confined to a few acres, I wish to decorate Kingdoms, even the world, & far from attending merely to the narrow views of selfish individuals, I would diffuse the comforts of cultivation to all mankind." Jean-Pierre Le Dantec in *Jardins et paysages,* 193, suggests that the "English artist" is probably Whately.

24. Watelet employs here similar imagery as that used by William Chambers to describe the horrid or terrifying character of Chinese gardens. See R. C. Bald, "Sir William Chambers and the Chinese Garden," who quotes from Chambers's *Miscellaneous Pieces,* 299 and 305. "Their enchanted scenes answer, in a great measure, to what we call romantic, and in these they make use of several artifices to excite surprise. Sometimes they make a rapid stream, or torrent, pass under ground, the turbulent noise of which strikes the ear of the newcomer, who is at a loss to know from whence it proceeds: at other times they dispose the rocks, buildings, and other objects that form the composition, in such a manner as that the wind passing through the different interstices and cavities, made in them for that purpose, causes strange and uncommon sounds. They introduce into these scenes all kinds of extraordinary trees, plants, and flowers, that form artificial and complicated ecchoes and let loose

different sorts of monstrous birds and animals. In their scenes of horror, they introduce impending rocks, dark caverns, and impetuous cataracts rushing down the mountains from all sides; the trees are ill-formed, and seemingly torn to pieces by the violence of tempests; some are thrown down, and intercept the course of the currents, appearing as if they had been brought down by the fury of the waters; others look as if shattered and blasted by the force of lightening; the buildings are some in ruins, others half-consumed by fire, and some miserable huts dispersed in the mountains serve, at once to indicate the existence and the wretchedness of the inhabitants. These scenes are generally succeeded by pleasing ones." Such scenes of terror included "gibbets, crosses, wheels, and the whole apparatus of torture," and, "to add both to the horror and sublimity of these scenes, they sometimes conceal in cavities, on the summits of the highest mountains, founderies, lime-kilns, and glass-works; which send forth large volumes of flame, and continued columns of thick smoke, that give to these mountains the appearance of volcanoes."

25. Sometimes, as here, Watelet uses "classe" to indicate a special social group, at other times he uses "état." I have used "class," although in 1774, date of the *Essay*'s publication, the term had not fully assumed its modern connotations. The *Dictionnaire de l'Académie Française* of 1798 defines "classe" in terms of merit and talent attributed to the members of certain professions: "a first class theologian, author, painter, etc." The 1835 edition of the *Dictionnaire*, however, states: "It is also used to mean orders, ranks that are established among men in society because of difference and inequality in their conditions: the various classes of society; high class; the middle class; the lower classes; the class of the poor; the class of artisans; the working class; all the classes of citizens."

26. An inhabitant of Sybaris, ancient Greek city in southern Italy, famed as a center of luxury and hedonism. Anyone very fond of self-indulgence and luxury; a voluptuary. Sybaris was destroyed in 510 B.C.

27. It should be understood that, in a stratified society such as that of the eighteenth century, Watelet is not aiming at its most powerful members, but rather at an aristocratic group with a very uncertain grip on power.

28. See Virgil, *The Aeneid*, book 6 (Aeneas's descent to the underworld).

29. In Greek and Roman mythology, Lethe, the river of forgetfulness, flows through Hades; its water produces loss of memory in those who drink of it.

30. See William Chambers, *Dissertation on Oriental Gardening*, which appeared in 1772, in both French and English. See Wiebenson, *Picturesque Garden in France*, 50–51.

31. R. C. Bald, in "Sir William Chambers and the Chinese Garden," 303, cites Chambers's comment on the partiality of the Chinese for artificial elements in their gardens: "They are fond of introducing statues, busts, bas-reliefs, and every production of the chisel, as well in other parts of their Gardens as around their buildings , . . . and they never fail to scatter ancient inscriptions, verses, and moral sentences, about their grounds; which are placed on large ruinated stones, and columns of marble, or engraved on trees or rocks." And Bald adds, "Inscriptions over garden doors or on pavilions are frequent in Chinese gardens, but it may be doubted whether they were ever 'engraved on trees,' in China or elsewhere, by anyone except vandals or sentimental trippers."

32. In Greek mythology, the dwelling place of virtuous people after death; any place or condition of ideal bliss or complete happiness.

33. Wiebenson, in *The Picturesque Garden in France*, 69, suggests that Watelet is

referring here to the "mausoleum" (in fact a memorial inscription) in honor of Signor Fido (a greyhound) on the rear of the Temple of the British Worthies in the Elysium Fields at Stowe, Buckinghamshire, England.

34. Ancient city on the coast of Cyprus. One of the earliest and most important centers of worship of Venus and the site of a famous temple to the goddess. She was thought to have been born of the sea-foam nearby.

35. Ancient city on the coast of Cyprus, sacred to Venus.

36. An enchantress who attracted men to her magic island and garden, made love to them, and then transformed them into rocks, streams, trees, waves, or wild beasts; she succeeded in seducing Ruggiero, who was eventually rescued from her charms, thus Alcina's power over all men was destroyed. See Ariosto, *Orlando furioso* (1516–1532).

37. A Saracen girl, a sorceress, in love with Rinaldo; she held him prisoner in her castle and enchanted gardens, away from the crusaders' army. See Torquato Tasso, *Gerusalemme liberata* (1580). (Watelet did a translation of this poem.)

38. See note 26.

39. This can be achieved by the use of a ha-ha—a moat or ditch, used in place of a fence, wall, or hedge, set around a garden, park, or private property without impairing the view or scenic appeal. Hirschfeld, in *The Theory of Garden Art*, 337, places great importance on the invention of the ha-ha. In his critique of Le Nôtre's "tiresome symmetry," he includes the following, taken from Horace Walpole: "But the capital stroke, the leading step to all that has followed, was the destruction of walls for boundaries, and the invention of *fossés*—an attempt then deemed so astonishing, that the common people called them Ha! Ha's! to express their surprize at finding a sudden and unperceived check to their walk. . . . No sooner was this simple enchantment made, than levelling, mowing and rolling, followed. The contiguous ground of the park without the sunk fence was to be harmonized with the lawn within; and the garden in its turn was to be set free from its prim regularity, that it might assort with the wilder country without." The idea of the ha-ha is a constant in many French garden treatises, including the work of Dézallier d'Argenville.

40. Sima Guang (1019–1086), Song dynasty Confucian scholar, statesman, and poet. He compiled the monumental study, *Comprehensive Mirror for Aid in Government*, a general chronicle of Chinese history from 403 B.C. to A.D. 959, considered one of the finest single historical works in Chinese. After a long and turbulent political career, he withdrew, in 1071, to his property, "The Garden of Solitary Pleasure" (De Le Yuan), at Luoyang, Henan province. His description of his garden is considered an important element in the history of Chinese garden literature. Watelet's "The Chinese Garden," although longer and more elaborate than Sima Guang's account, is clearly based on a translation of Sima's original. Unfortunately, it has been impossible to ascertain where Watelet obtained a French rendition of the Chinese text. Dora Wiebenson suggests in *The Picturesque Garden in* France, 69, note 53, that Watelet's "Chinese Garden" is not taken from Sima but from a garden description of another author, Liu Zhou (514–565), translated from the Chinese by P. M. Cibot (1727–1781), missionary in China, in his "Essai sur les jardins de plaisance des Chinois" ("Essay on the Pleasure Gardens of the Chinese"). This essay dates from the early 1770s and was later published in the collection *Mémoires concernant l'histoire, les sciences, les arts, les mœurs, les usages, &c, des Chinois: par les missionnaires de Pékin* (*Memoirs*

Concerning the History, the Sciences, the Arts, the Mores, the Customs, etc., of the Chinese: by the Missionaries of Peking), vol. 8: 301–326. Cibot quotes a lengthy statement by Liu Zhou on gardens in general, but there is no description in it of a private garden. For an English translation of Sima Guang's text, see Edwin T. Morris, *The Gardens of China: History, Art, and Meanings* (New York: Charles Scribner's Sons, 1983), 80–81, adapted from Osvald Sirén, *Gardens of China* (New York: Ronald Press, 1949).

41. Sima Guang reports that his library contained five thousand volumes.

42. The Yangtze River.

43. A stringed instrument, a lute.

44. See note 40.

45. In *Theory of Garden Art*, 87–92, Hirschfeld cites this chapter almost in its entirety. He prefaces this section with the following: "The clever scribblers of France have begun ridiculing the old symmetrical manner; enthusiasts glorify their imagined vision of the Chinese taste; experts follow nature and the English manner as they seek the principles to create gardens more beautiful than those of their ancestors. People are now busy laying out gardens or improving old ones in a purer taste. There is one man familiar with the fine arts whose own daily life reflects the taste and philosophy manifest in his writings, and he has given us a garden description so pleasant that it will certainly delight the connoisseur. This is a model for the French nation of a modest and delightfully pastoral garden. I would find more pleasure in a lovely spring day spent here in the company of its owner, Mr. Watelet, than in all the splendor and festivity of Versailles."

46. Gaius Plinius Caecilius Secundus (ca. A.D. 62–ca. 113) was a Roman writer particularly famous for his letters, which offer an important portrayal of the society of his time. In letter 2.17, addressed to Clusinius (?) Gallus, Pliny describes in considerable detail his villa and garden, the Laurentine, on the coast, seventeen miles southwest of Rome, near Ostia: "Miraris cur me Laurentinum vel (si ita mavis), Laurens meum tanto opere delectet; desines mirari, cum cognoveris gratiam villae, opportunitatem loci, litoris spatium." "You may wonder why my Laurentine place (or my Laurentian, if you like that better) is such a joy to me, but once you realize the attractions of the house itself, the amenities of its situation, and its extensive seafront, you will have your answer." Pliny, *Letters and Panegyricus*, trans. Betty Radice, Loeb Classical Library (Cambridge, Mass.: Harvard University Press, 1969), vol. 1, book 2, letter 17, pp. 132–133.

47. The city of Paris.

48. The Seine River.

49. Watelet discovered the site for his future estate shortly before 1750. For further information see Françoise Arquié-Bruley's exhaustively researched and informative article "Watelet, Marguerite Le Comte et le Moulin joli d'après les Archives nationales," *Bulletin de la Société de l'Histoire de l'Art français*, Année 1998 (1999): 131–156.

50. Approximately one third of a mile.

51. This was no doubt a private joke between Watelet and the Le Comte couple, for although Watelet purchased Moulin Joli, he was only a "resident" there; for unknown reasons, Mme Le Comte and her husband were named legal owners of the estate. See Françoise Arquié-Bruley, "Watelet, Marguerite Le Comte

et le Moulin joli d'après les Archives Nationales," *Bulletin de la Société de l'Histoire de l'Art français,* Année 1998 (1999), 131–156.

52. Most probably the painter François Boucher (1703–1770).

53. It is not quite clear what Watelet means by "just as we know of someone who once became a painter out of love," for his elliptical French could be understood in various ways. He may be making a cryptic remark about Boucher, which is doubtful, or he could be making, through Boucher, an oblique reference to himself, for he was, among other things, also an engraver, painter, and sculptor. He may be suggesting that earlier in life he became an artist in order to paint his "love," Marguerite Le Comte, with whom he lived, with her husband's consent, for some thirty years, in a very civilized and comfortable ménage à trois, first in Paris, then in the country. I know of one portrait of Marguerite Le Comte by Watelet and of an engraving by Louis-Simon Lempereur based on that portrait.

54. This is how Le Prince de Ligne describes his visit to Moulin Joli: "One day, abandoning the vain whirl of the capital and following my own whimsy, I lost sight of Paris at Moulin Joli and found myself (possibly only in Nature). Whoever you may be, unless your heart is hardened, sit down in the fork of a willow by the riverside at Moulin Joli. Read, look around, and weep—not from sadness but from a delicious feeling of sensibility. The panorama of your soul will appear before you. Past happiness (should you have known it), happiness to come, and the desire to be happy—a thousand thoughts revolving around this one thought, regrets, joys, desires, all will rush upon you at once. Struggles . . . your indignation . . . the heart . . . memories . . . the present . . . Go away, unbelievers! Reflect upon the inscriptions that Taste has placed there. Meditate with the wise man, sigh with the lover, and bless M. Watelet." Prince Charles Joseph de Ligne, *Coup d'Œil at Belœil,* 188–189.

55. Again, De Ligne in *Coup d'Œil at Belœil,* 189: "I have never seen anything quite like the two bridges at Moulin Joli. The Dutch bridge, leading to the second island, and the other, which is a suspension bridge edged with flowers, have a fairy-tale quality. Yet the treatment is not reasonable, for there is no explanation why there should be cases, shrubs, and the semblance of orange trees. But it is the prettiest unreason in the world. These non sequiturs par excellence are the specialty of the Chinese."

56. A sitting room or parlor.

57. I have been unable to identify the authors of the poetic fragments cited in this chapter. They may have been composed by Watelet himself or by some of his many guests on the occasion of a visit to Moulin Joli—in particular, by his protégé the poet Antoine-Léonard Thomas or by l'abbé Delille (Jacques Delille), a nature poet and author of the poem *Les Jardins* (1782). In an article reviewing *Essai sur les jardins,* F. M. Grimm, echoing Watelet, writes, "This last piece, the one I liked the best, is a very faithful and meticulous description of Moulin Joli. We only noticed that the poetic inscriptions—which one comes upon with pleasure in the garden for which they were made—had lost much for being put into print, and are like fruit that is only pleasing if it is picked on the tree that produced it." F. M. Grimm, *Correspondance littéraire, philosophique et critique par Grimm, Diderot, Raynal, Meister, etc.,* ed. M. Tourneux, (Paris: Garnier Frères, 1877–1882), vol. 10, December 1774, 522.

58. In Greek mythology, a Hamadryad is a dryad, specifically a wood nymph; she is supposed to be born and die with the tree she inhabits.

59. I.e., Watelet, Marguerite Le Comte, her husband, and their friends.

60. No doubt, the Benedictine abbey at Argenteuil, near Watelet's property. It was destroyed during the French Revolution.

61. Héloïse (1101–1164) was the brilliant pupil of Pierre Abélard, whom she secretly married and by whom she had a son, named Astrolabe. Forced in disgrace to be separated from Abélard, she entered the Benedictine convent at the abbey of Argenteuil. After the convent was dispersed, Abélard gave Héloïse and her nuns the property of the community of the Paraclete, near Nogent-sur-Seine, which he had been allowed to found. There Héloïse became abbess. She exchanged with Abélard a lengthy correspondence containing themes of piety, scholasticism, and amorous passion.

62. Pierre Abélard (1079–1142), a brilliant and controversial theologian and philosopher. A famous dialectician opposed to the application of realism in the discussion of universals, Abélard was condemned, at the instigation of Saint Bernard, for his doctrine concerning the nature of the Trinity. Secretly married to his pupil Heloïse, he was castrated by order of the canon Fulbert, Héloïse's uncle. Abélard then embraced the monastic life at the royal abbey of Saint-Denis near Paris and made the unwilling Héloïse become a nun at the convent of Argenteuil.

63. Abélard was never abbot at Argenteuil. He was, however, abbot at the convent of the Paraclete, where Héloïse was abbess, and provided it with a rule and with a justification of the nun's way of life; in this he emphasized the virtue of literary study.

64. Soon after Watelet's death—too soon, some thought—Marguerite Le Comte, put Moulin Joli up for sale, but found no buyers because of the exorbitant amount she was asking for it. Madame de Sabran (possibly the same as in Rousseau's *Confessions*) offered to buy it; she finally gave up, but not without writing, "Madame Le Comte, who spent there many a happy day in the arms of love, considers it priceless, and would have me pay for all her pleasures!" Charles Alexandre de Calonne, controller general of finances, wished to acquire the property for his mistress, the painter Madame Vigée-Lebrun, but the deal fell through. Marguerite Le Comte owned the place until her death. During the French Revolution, it was bought by a merchant who cut down the trees, parceled the land, and sold it piecemeal. Nothing remains today of Moulin Joli, one of the most famous gardens in Europe and one visited in its prime by the major French and international figures of a generation, including Louis XVI and Marie-Antoinette, numerous artists, composers, politicians, and academicians, many of the *philosophes,* and even Benjamin Franklin, in 1777. See Maurice Henriet, "Un Amateur d'art au XVIIIe siècle: L'Académicien Watelet," *Gazette des Beaux-Arts* (September-October 1922): 173–194.

Bibliography

WRITINGS BY CLAUDE-HENRI WATELET

Essai sur les jardins. Paris, 1774. Reprinted in facsimile by Minkoff Press, Geneva, 1972. [The 1774 edition appeared in two different impressions. Both are dated 1774 and have the same text, but are different in publisher's name, ornamental space fillers, and censor's dates. One impression—"Chez Prault"—bears the censor's date November 11, 1774; the other—"Chez Prault, Saillant, Nyon, Pissot"—bears the censor's date of November 21, 1774. The Minkoff edition is of the "later" imprint.]

Art-Related Works

L'Art de peindre. Poëme. Avec des réflexions sur les différentes parties de la peinture. Paris: H. L. Guérin and L.-F. Delatour, 1760. [New edition. Amsterdam: aux dépens de la Compagnie, 1761.]
L'Arte della pittura, poema con alcune Riflessioni . . . Translated by Agostino Lomellini. Genoa: P. & A. Scionico, 1765.
L'Arte della pittura, . . . Translated by Gasparo Gozzi. Venice: M. Fenzo, 1771.
Dictionnaire des beaux-arts. Completed by Pierre-Charles Lévesque. 2 vols. Paris: Panckoucke, 1788–1791.
Dictionnaire des arts de peinture, sculpture et gravure. Completed by Pierre-Charles Lévesque. 5 vols. Paris: L.-F. Prault, 1792.

Several theater pieces, many of which were published in 1784 in a collection by L.-F. Prault. When known, dates of composition are in parentheses.

Silvie. London, 1743.
Zénéïde. Paris: Prault, 1784. (1743)
La Vallée de Tempé. The Hague: J. Neaume, 1747; Paris: Prault, 1784.
Délie. Paris: Prault, 1784. (1765)
Deucalion et Pyrrha. Paris: P.-F. Gueffier, 1772. (1765)
Les Statuaires d'Athènes. Paris: Prault, 1784. (1766)
La Maison de campagne à la mode, ou la Comédie d'après nature. Paris: Prault, 1784. (1777)
Phaon. Paris: P.-R.-C. Ballard, [n.d.]; Paris: Prault, 1784. (1778)
Milon. Paris: Prault, 1784.

Pygmalion. Paris: Prault, 1784.
Les Veuves, ou la Matrône d'Éphèse. Paris: Prault, 1784.

BOOKS AND ARTICLES

Arquié-Bruley, Françoise. "Watelet, Marguerite Le Comte et le Moulin joli d'après les Archives nationales." *Bulletin de la Société de l'Histoire de l'Art français.* Année 1998 (1999).

Bald, R. C. "Sir William Chambers and the Chinese Garden." *Journal of the History of Ideas* 10, no. 3 (June 1950).

Baridon, Michel. *Les Jardins: Paysagistes—jardiniers—poètes.* Paris: Robert Laffont, 1998.

Cayeux, Jean de. "Watelet et Rembrandt." *Bulletin de la Société de l'Histoire de l'Art français.* Année 1965 (1966): 131–160.

Cibot, P. M. "Essai sur les jardins de plaisance des Chinois." *Mémoires concernant l'histoire, les sciences, les arts, les mœurs, les usages, etc., des Chinois: par les missionnaires du Pékin.* Paris: Nyon, 1782.

Collette, Florence, and Denise Péricard-Méa, eds. *Le Temps des jardins.* Conseil général de Seine-et-Marne, 1992.

Conan, Michel. *Dictionnaire historique de l'art des jardins.* Paris: Hazan, 1997.

Couffy, Annick, ed. *Jardins en Val d'Oise.* Conseil général du Val d'Oise, 1993.

Dictionnaire de l'Académie Française, editions of 1694, 1798, 1835.

Dictionnaire historique de la langue française, sous la direction de Alain Rey. Paris: Dictionnaires Le Robert, 1992.

Ganay, Ernest de. *Bibliographie de l'art des jardins.* Edited with a biographical essay by M. Mosser. Paris: Union des Arts Décoratifs, 1989.

Girardin, René Louis, marquis de. *De la composition des paysages, ou des moyens d'embellir la nature autour des habitations en joignant l'agréable à l'utile.* Geneva, 1777. English translation by D. Malthus, *An Essay on Landscape; or, on the means of improving and embellishing the country round our habitations.* London, 1783. Reprint of the Malthus translation by Garland Publishers, 1982.

Grimm, F. M. *Correspondance littéraire, philosophique et critique par Grimm, Diderot, Raynal, Meister, etc.* Edited by Maurice Tourneux. Paris: Garnier Frères, 1877–1882.

Guillemard, Colette. *Les Mots des parcs et des jardins.* Paris: Editions Belin, 2001.

Henriet, Maurice. "Un Amateur d'art au XVIIIe siècle. L'Académicien Watelet." *Gazette des Beaux-Arts* (September-October 1922): 173–194.

Hirschfeld, C. C. L. *Theory of Garden Art.* Edited and translated by Linda B. Parshall. Philadelphia: University of Pennsylvania Press, 2001.

Hofer, Philip. *A Visit to Rome in 1764.* Cambridge: Harvard College, 1956.

Hogarth, William. *The Analysis of Beauty.* Edited with an introduction and notes by Ronald Paulson. New Haven: Yale University Press, 1997.

Homer. *The Odyssey.* Translated by Robert Fitzgerald. New York: Doubleday, 1961.

Hunt, John Dixon. "Emblem and Expression in the Eighteenth-Century Landscape Garden." In *Gardens and the Picturesque: Studies in the History of Landscape Architecture.* Cambridge, Mass.: MIT Press, 1992.

———. *The Picturesque Garden in Europe.* New York: Thames & Hudson, 2002.

Lavin, Sylvia. "Sacrifice and the Garden: Watelet's *Essai sur les jardins* and the Space of the Picturesque." *Assemblage* 28 (1996): 16–33.

Le Dantec, Jean-Pierre. *Jardins et paysages—Textes crtiques de l'antiquité à nos jours.* Paris: Larousse, 1996.

Le Ménahèze, Sophie. *L'Invention du jardin romantique en France, 1761–1808.* Preface by Michel Baridon. Neuilly-sur-Seine: Editions Spiralinthe, 2001.

Ligne, Prince Charles Joseph de. *Coup d'Œil at Belœil and a Great Number of European Gardens.* Translated and edited by Basil Guy. Berkeley: University of California Press, 1991.

Magnol-Malhache, V., and G. Weill, eds. *Jardins et paysages des Hauts-de-Seine.* Nanterre, 1982.

Malecot, Yves, ed. *Jardins en France, 1760–1820: Pays d'illusion, Terre d'expérience.* Preface by Jurgis Baltrusaitis. Caisse nationale des Monuments Historiques et des Sites. Paris, 1977.

Middleton, Robin. Introduction. Nicolas Le Camus de Mézières, *The Genius of Architecture; or, The Analogy of that Art with Our Sensations.* Translated by David Britt. Santa Monica, Calif.: Getty Center for the History of Art and the Humanities, 1992.

Morris, Edwin T. *The Gardens of China: History, Art, and Meanings.* New York: Charles Scribner's Sons, 1983.

Pliny the Younger. *Letters and Panegyricus.* English translation by Betty Radice. Loeb Classical Library. Cambridge, Mass.: Harvard University Press, 1969.

Ratouis de Limay, Paul. *Un Amateur orléanais au XVIIIe siècle. Aignan-Thomas Desfriches.* Paris: Librairie H. Champion, 1907.

Roddier, H. Appendix IV, "Rousseau et le Marquis de Girardin ou Comment l'Art des jardins conduit du *Romanesque* au *Romantisme.*" In J. J. Rousseau, *Les Rêveries du promeneur solitaire.* Edited by H. Roddier. Paris: Garnier, 1997.

Roland, Charles-Nicolas. *Mémoire au Roi Louis XVI, ou Journal de mes emprisonnemens à la Bastille.* London, 1784.

Rousseau, Jean-Jacques. *Les Rêveries du promeneur solitaire.* Edited by H. Roddier. Paris: Garnier, 1997.

Saint Girons, Baldine. *Esthétique du XVIIIe siècle: Le modèle français.* Paris: P. Sers, 1990.

Vicq-d'Azyr, Félix. *Œuvres de Vicq-d'Azyr . . .* Compiled and annotated by Jacques L. Moreau. Paris: L. Duprat-Duverger, l'an XIII—1805. [Contains eulogy delivered by Vicq-d'Azyr for Watelet at the Académie française. Reprinted in the *Dictionnaire des beaux-arts* of Panckoucke's *Encyclopédie méthodique.* Paris, 1788–1791.]

Virgil. *Eclogues, Georgics, Aeneid 1–6.* Translated by H. Rushton Fairclough, revised by G. P. Goold. Loeb Classical Library, Cambridge, Mass.: Harvard University Press, 1999.

Wiebenson, Dora. *The Picturesque Garden in France.* Princeton: Princeton University Press, 1978.

Index

Acknowledgments

I am grateful to Reed College for the generous support it has provided with released time and resources.

Many colleagues and friends helped in various ways with this project and I want to express my appreciation to them: Michel Baridon, Doris Desclais Berkvam, William Diebold, Basil Guy, Hugh Hochman, John Dixon Hunt, Leonard Johnson, Raymond Kierstead, Michel Lanoote, Nigel Nicholson, Pascal Ponsart-Ponsart, William Ray, Hyong Rhew, Charlene Woodcock, Charles Wu. I am particularly indebted to Roger Porter for having come to the rescue of many a convoluted sentence and to Peter Parshall for assistance with bibliography and iconography.

This project, however, would not have been possible without the friendship and support of Linda B. Parshall and Samuel N. Rosenberg. They read various versions of the manuscript, provided much needed editorial advice, and offered constant encouragement. This small book is dedicated to them.

S. D.